THE BOY IN
THE MIDDLE

THE BOY IN THE MIDDLE

And The Amazing Grace of God

Robert Harris

To order additional copies of this book, contact:
Xlibris Corporation
1-888-795-4274
www.Xlibris.com
Orders@Xlibris.com
39164

CONTENTS

Dedication

I want to first dedicate this book to my father Robert Harris Jr. and my father-in-law William P. Chapman, who are both deceased. They taught me well and I appreciate every minute of their teachings. I also send thanks out to my dearest mother Thomasina Harris, who wouldn't give up on me. Last but not least, my oldest daughter Tonya Harris, who helped me diligently at the end and my baby daughter Jade Harris. And my other two daughters Crystal and Melody, who came back on my side.

FOREWORD

This book is a most unusual book than others, simply because it identifies true, real life issues that occurs in some people lives, that's never told. This particular story involves a young kid who wanted a destiny above his own imagination and situation. But through life he made wrong choices that caused him more harm than good. Regardless, of all the setbacks and mistakes he made for himself, he kept pressing toward a mark he never could see until his heavenly Father opened his eyes.

I Robert E. Harris, wrote this book fully inspired from the Holy Spirit, hoping that whoever reads this book will be enlightened to another dimension of understanding. God had me write about this story of how He brought me out of the horrible pit and set my feet on a Solid Rock. God had Prophets write about how He talked to them and how He had a relationship with His servants. There were Adam, Abraham, Moses, Elijah and many more. God still speaks to us today and desires to have a one on one relationship with us. But some people think that God doesn't talk or relate to us anymore and believe, that was then and this is now. I am a living witness and will stand on top of Mt. Everett and tell the whole world that God is real and is still very much alive.

This book tells the story of what happened in the belly of the whale, sort of speaking. The story was told about Jonah before and after he was in the belly of the whale. But never while he was in the whale, so I'm bringing the news on what goes on in the belly of the whale. We all have to go through a process to be a faithful servant of our Father God. So through the Holy Spirit, I'm sharing with everybody my experience in the process.

I give God all the Glory for this project because He took an unlearned man, who have never been to college or seminary and poured His Spirit in me to be able to write about the Deliverance and the Transformation He(God) performed in my life. God said in His Word that in the last days, He will pour His Spirit in all flesh. If we tap into God's Amazing Grace, He will open your eyes to a destiny you could never imagine. He said in His Word, there's nothing impossible for Him.

My biggest hope is to deliver this book in every prison camp in America. And that it will touch every heart that set eyes on it. That this book will give hope to all who feels hopeless, worthless and in despair. The scenes in this book can identify with just about every walk of life. God is no respect of person. He always has His hand stretched out for us to come.

I truly believe, people like Apostle Paul wrote for God, things he experienced for himself and endured trials, tests and tribulations, in order to write the unsearchable things of God.

Through this ministry, God enabled me to relate to others, who have experienced similar things as I have. God have drawn men, women and teenage boys to me to witness and to share my testimony with. Some are in the streets and some are already incarcerated. I have a few letters to share, I wrote to a young man that's incarcerated:

Hey Shon, how are you doing, very well I hope. You really blessed my soul by hearing from you because I was just thinking about your situation right at the same time you sent me the letter. You just gave me confirmation to what to do. I enjoy listening to you and your life in there, maybe if you tell me enough, I'll write a book about your story. That's what I'm trying to ease into but it's not easy. God is really helping me on my first book and by His Grace, I believe it can be done. I'm almost finished though, if I ever find more time to write. It helps me express myself more clearly to the world. I want you to know that I don't mind sharing funds with you as long as you are for some serious business with your life. To me life is too valuable to be wasted on nothing. We have to learn to push ourselves to higher levels no matter what the situation may be, especially being a Black man in America or anywhere else. Yeah, we had some setbacks but that don't give us the excuse to give up. As long as I have breath, I'm gonna fight with my last breath. The devil tries to steal our lives and he tries to keep us in despair and the sad thing about it is, society seems to be on the devil side. That's why, I need God because it's to much to battle with by myself, so if God is the higher power, I want some of that power too. And the only way I can get some of that power is to learn what God likes and dislikes and find out what I have to do to get some of this power. I tell you, it hasn't been an easy road but I haven't gave up neither, I came close but every time I look back to what I've been through, it makes me stronger to go even further. I'm telling you not to give up even when things look hopeless, just hold on we're not off the cliff yet and maybe help is right around the corner. I personally don't know you but I think I can tell you something I want you to do. Turn your situation around by getting to yourself, reading good material that will teach you in the mind and in the heart. Something that will give you life, beyond the ordinary. Don't tell me you can't do it because I've seen illiterate people climb these mountains, especially with the help of God. Then before you know it, you'll be, not only taught but will be able to teach. I don't know what is your greatest desire and maybe you don't neither but once you grow in life's material, which is to me is God's Book. I know you might get weary of it because you can't understand it, that's why I said get books that will teach you in the mind, to tackle Life's Obstacles. The reason why I keep pushing this knowledge in you is because my biggest hope is to see you develop into the person God intend for you to be and to make you all over again so you can bring full joy in your mother's heart. But you gots to want it for yourself first and not for nobody else. I want to leave you with this note, you don't ever have to pay me back, no matter how much money I send you. Like I say, my biggest hope is to see you a New Man. This is the time for you to show up and to show out and in doing so I guarantee, you'll be out before seven years. The faster you develop the faster you'll be out, believe that. I'm not telling you something I haven't experienced for myself. And you know what, I'm glad God changed me and made me new again. I lost a few friends, even while I was in jail but I gained a few too, even to the point of following me because they were looking for something pure too. Oh yeah, thank you for the kite.

Love You, Robert Earl

Dear Shon, it's me again, sitting here thinking about you. I been had you on my mind for a while, wondering if you are still holding everything in the road. It's a new year now and you suppose to be trying to do everything different and better than you did last year, people say. They say leave the past behind and keep moving forward. But after you get over the hype of bringing in the New Year, then what's next. Everything you saw last year is still staring you in the face this year. So what do we do? The guy that lived next door to me was thirty seven or thirty eight years old and the last time I seen him was Friday and he died Sunday on New Years eve. It kind of shocked me, because he looked okay to me when I saw him but we never know. You know sometimes life deals you a dirty hand and you wrestled with them dirty hands for a long while. I know a lot of people done checked out of here and never got a chance to clean their selves up. And I know some people who don't care if they ever clean their hands up. Which one is better? The one who never got a chance or the one who don't care or the one who keep on trying no matter what it look like. They say only the strong survive but what do they know. Some try to tell you what to do, if you are stranded in an ocean and some try to tell you what to do if you are left in the desert but what do they know, they never been there before.

You know, you may think about all the things you might do when you get out, saying to yourself, the world want be able to hold me once I hit the pavement again. Then when you get out and see that there's more people are locked up in the minds of their own prison. Then you run for a little while because you are physically free until it hit you that you are not free at all. The same things you've did before, you repeats year after year after year. No matter how long you stay away, that circle is still there somewhere. How can you break the circle and break free? Even some Christian folks are locked up in their own prison. Because they can't see outside of their own little minds, so they gets comfortable until the day they die. Everybody is doing the same old thing, day after day. It's uncommon to do anything different than the ordinary. Until you see someone else break that circle and make it, first. Then you may say, if they made it, then I might can make it too. But who knows, you maybe the first to break that circle. They say only the strong survive but what do they know!

THE SKY IS THE LIMIT; YOU ARE A KING; WALK AS A KING; THEY CALL YOU DAWG NOW; ONE DAY THEY WILL CALL YOU MR. SHON; QUIT THINKING SMALL; THINK BIG; BE HUMBLE WITHOUT FEAR; TALK TO THE PRESIDENT JUST LIKE YOU TALK TO THE JANITOR; TALK TO THE JANITOR JUST LIKE YOU TALK TO THE PRESIDENT:

I love you Shon so hang in there, oh yeah, I'll try to send you some paper next week.

Dear Shon, it's me again, your friend Robert Earl. I just want to check on you and see how you are doing. I haven't had a chance to send you anything yet but something should be coming your way shortly after you receive this letter. Keep me in your prayers so that my finances can pick up and then maybe I can help you more as God wills. I pray for you constantly hoping that you are getting your heart right. Whenever you pray, please don't pray against anyone no matter what they have did to you. God has a rule in His Bible that stands in the entire world and that rule is you reap what you sow. No matter what you sow it has to come back to you in some form or fashion. I've learned to sow good seed in just about everything I can possibly do. Because that rule do stand. Oh yeah, before I leave you, I want you if possible to write something like a journal or a story about your life and how you've felt inside over the years until now. If you don't have the time or rather not re-live it, then please forgive me for mentioning it. Stay in perfect peace, I'll be seeing you real soon. One more thing, please let me know if I can use these letters in my book.

INTRODUCTION

Hey Shon, this is your friend Robert Harris checking on you, wondering how you are doing. I haven't talk with you in a while and I ask you for forgiveness of my slackness. I hope you are keeping your head up and thinking positive no matter what the situation may be or may seemed. Our faith are not what we see but what we believe deep down in our soul. You may say I don't understand or see what you are going through but secretly I feel your pain and agony at times. So I just want to drop some real stuff on you, I hope will motivate you to another whole level, not a half of a level but a whole:

> Our deepest fear is not that we are inadequate
> Our deepest fear is that we are powerful beyond measure.
>
> We ask ourselves who am I to be brilliant, gorgeous, talented and fabulous.
> Actually who are you not to be, we were born to make manifested the glory of God that is within us.
> And as we let our own light shine we unconsciously give other people permission to do the same.

Please take this letter and tie it around your neck of remembrance that your understanding will be enlightened so you can go forward with full joy and full confidence. I want to take you just a little deeper, so just hold on: First, King David from the Old Testament made a great sin in the sight of the Lord and he repented to the Lord in Psalms 51. Please don't stop reading because you might can help someone else with this same letter. In Psalms 51, David did a lot of explaining but the most exhilarating words that caught my attention was when he said, Restore to me the joy of Your salvation and uphold me by Your Spirit. Again I say Restore unto me a joy, I want to speak to you about joy, Salvation Joy.

There are affects of joy, joy comes from many things. In the natural joy is a strong feeling of happiness, a state or source of contentment or satisfaction.

Anything which makes one delighted or happy. Joy is good like a medicine. If you can smile and be glad its good for the heart. For there are many things to cause you to have joy. For instance, in the natural world joy comes from accomplishments and achievements. From any level, when someone achieves something it makes them extremely joyful. Not only does it makes them joyful but it makes the people who knows the person joyful. I use to enjoy watching Michael Jordan, when he use to play the game of basketball with such intensity and grace. They tried to stop him but he was unstoppable. He brought love to the game of basketball. He also broke all kinds of unspeakable records, he made great achievements and was the Icon of basketball. He brought joy to the game and made a lot of people happy but that was in the world of basketball. In the world of political economics, everyone has achieved something and have made someone happy. Happiness to darkness has turned out a lot of people. Too many people are unhappy, you need to be happy. Be happy with your wife, be happy with your children and children be happy with your parents, sisters and brothers no matter what happened in the past. Happy, happy, happy, everybody needs to be happy.

I remembered once upon a time a lady said, when she first got married she was the happiest woman in the world but now she is the saddest woman in the world. This is true with so many people where happiness leaves, in fact, it's hard to retain. But there is a happiness I want to talk to you about, a joy I want to talk to you about called Salvation joy. It's different than any other joy, when one is healed by the power of God there is a joy. Just to know you was healed by the power of God. There is another joy, when you've been fighting a long time and the Lord gives you the victory. It looked like you wasn't going to win but you came out on top. I tell you that's a joy, you can look back and say, look where God have brought me from. Then there's another joy that comes out of being tempted. You feel like you gonna yield to that temptation, you feel like this one is going to do you in. And all of a sudden, God turns the table and gives you the victory, hallelujah, praise His name. That kind of joy sets you on fire because the devil thought he had you but now you'll standing on cloud nine, saying He's able to keep what I have committed unto that day. Then another joy comes out of praying through until you know God is listening to you, until you feel it in your heart, until you feel it in your soul, that your prayers are being heard in glory. Until your countenance change, until the substances of your soul becomes satisfied. I tell you that's a joy, hallelujah thank you Jesus. There's another joy, when people organize against you and you know they are planning your destruction. You know they are planning your defeat, you know they are planning to do you in but then all of a sudden God turns the table. God steps into your situation and gives you the victory. I tell you it brings joy to your soul and peace to your mind. Then you can look at satan and say ha-ha, praise the Lord. Victory, victory shall be mine, victory, victory shall be mine. If I hold my peace and let the Lord fight my battles victory, victory shall be mine.

Then there comes another joy, that's called Salvation joy, the joy of being Saved. But there's a conversion joy because I was converted before I got the Holy Spirit. I'll never forget it the night I was walking thru the woods something like a jungle. On my way to revival because didn't nobody wanted to go to church so I decided to go by myself. When I was out there in them woods, I was forced to pray because it was dark and I was only nine years old. I didn't know it was so many sounds in the bush at night time. So I thought, I better start praying, when I started praying something happen to me. All my fears of what was in the bush went away, something came to me like a light from the Glory of God. I felt so peaceful and calm, when I reached church that night I knew I had been converted. I knew the Lord had touch me, that was conversion joy, that wasn't Salvation joy that wasn't Holy Ghost joy. I didn't know there was another joy other than conversion joy. I thought that was it, only to discover that the joy that comes with Salvation is a different kind of joy. Some joys are short lived and some joys are lasting joys, Salvation joy is a lasting joy. It's not a short lived joy, it doesn't die out it doesn't leave you in one day, it doesn't leave you in six months, it doesn't leave you in one year. Salvation joy is something you can keep forever and it'll get better and better and better. But the way you keep Salvation joy, you have to learn how to praise God because that's the way you received it, when you received salvation, by praising the Lord. You was saying hallelujah, thank you Jesus. And while you was praising Him, He came into your heart, into your soul, into your mind and into your spirit. he lifted you to heights you have never known before. When He did this to you, you knew at this time, this is it. No doubt about it, this is salvation, this is the Holy Spirit, this is tongue talking experience. From this very moment on you knew you had joy like a river, you had joy that nothing could take from you. It was so blessed, it was so assuring, it was so illuminating, it was so invigorating. It was a joy of lightness that no man had ever experience before.

Listen to these words of the Lord Jesus Christ in John 15:11, these things have I spoken to you that my joy may remain in you and that your joy may be full. The Lord want you to have a full cup of joy not a half of cup. In John 16: 24 Jesus said, until now you have asked nothing in My name, ask and you will receive that your joy may be full. These scriptures relates to a full joy, we've lost some joy and we want the Lord to give it back to us, we want a full joy. How do you acquire this full joy? By learning to do what you did when you received the gift of the Holy Spirit and that's praising the Lord. If the world really knew how real the Holy Spirit really are, they wouldn't fight it. No way would you fight the gift of the Holy Spirit, there wouldn't be a Bishop in anybody's church without the Holy Spirit. That's why I like to see everybody try it, every Bishop that's against it try it. I guaranteed you that your life will become illuminated by the power of God. I guarantee you there will come a joy into your heart and a peace into your soul and a lightness you have never seen before. I tell you there's a joy in Christianity, there is a joy knowing you are a child of God and knowing the wonderful salvation that comes from our Lord and our Savior Jesus Christ.

King David had lost his joy, he lost it because of sin. And sin will do it everytime, it will take your joy. Sin will take your joy and leave you flat, and I don't want nothing to leave me flat. I wanna be picked up, life needs a pick up, life is too much of a burden to be left flat. Life is too complicated, life is too depressive, life is too oppressed to be left flat. Give me something that's gonna pick me up and hold me up. David became flat in his spiritual life and lost his joy. And when you lose your joy you don't wanna go to church no more, you go out of tradition you go out of the fact, you don't want nobody to know you done lost your joy. But ohh! when you lose your joy, it's a burden to you, it's a depressing feeling, I know because I been there, I know where you are, when it comes to losing your joy. I didn't lose my joy because of sin, I lost my joy because of problems. Problems can beat you to the ground, problems will beat you to the ground. I had reached the point one time, when I didn't wanna go to church, problems just beated me to the ground. But in the midst of my suffering, I discovered there's a suffering joy, praise the name of God, hallelujah. There is a joy that comes out of suffering that I didn't know about, praise the name of God. When I reached rock bottom or should I say flat to the ground. I felt like I didn't feel nothing anymore, felt like I didn't have nothing anymore, felt like nobody loved me anymore, felt like nobody cared. In the midst of those situations I decided to cry out to God Almighty. And I started crying and crying and crying, I cried one night from the midnight until the sun rose the next morning. When the sun rose, it brought a joy into my soul, it brought a peace into my mind, like I never seen before. I know now, there's a joy that comes out of suffering and its better than any joy that I know about. If you ever get suffering joy, you can hold on to whatever, praise the Lord. No matter what comes against you, you can hang in there, ohh yes you can. No matter who abused you, no matter who talks about you, you can hang in there because you've come to a place in God. Weeping may endure for a night but joy cometh in the morning.

King David had lost his joy he was flat, he had no joy in his soul, he had no joy in his mind. And when a saint loses his Salvation joy it's a miserable state of mind. David said to himself, I'm going after my joy, ohh yes I am, I'm gonna tell the Lord, I want my joy back. I've been trying to get it back being a hypocrite but that won't bring my joy back, I've been trying to justify myself as of what I had done as being alright. But that won't bring my joy back neither. So, what I'm going to do now is tell the truth and see will this get my joy back. I'm gonna tell it like it is, I'm not going to be a hypocrite no more, I'm gonna be for real. I'm gonna tell God, I have sinned, yes I have, I have committed a terrible sin and I know that I'm guilty and I know that You (God) have something against me. Then David said, Lord I want you to do something for me, if I repent, I want You to give me something. Something I had a long time ago, I want you to give me something I use to have but I don't have it anymore. I have fellowship with the nation of Europe, I have fellowship with the nation of Africa, I have fellowship with nations of Asia Minor, I have fellowship with the Palestinian nations. But ohh God, I don't have Your fellowship, everybody are talking to me except You God. I want You God to come into my life, I want to be able to call You anytime, the way I used to. I used to talk to You God in the back woods, I used to talk to You when I was a shepherd boy. I used to sing and You use to bless my singing, I used to praise Your name and You used to bless my heart. But since I lost my joy, I haven't got no song and I haven't got no peace, I'm living in hell every night. David said, Lord I want You to search my heart, yes I do, You God knows the heart of every man, You know what's wrong and You know what's right. You God, know what's crooked and You know what's straight and You know my heart. I want You to search me, shine a light from heaven on my soul. If You find anything that shouldn't be, take it out. I want You to get rid of it for me because I want my joy back.

I want to shout again, I want to run, I want to clap my hands and pat my feet. I want to play my musical instrument, I wanna be glad in my heart, I wanna be glad in my soul. Ohh Lord fix my heart, fix my soul, fix me, I got to be fixed, I used to be fixed but something happened to me, fix me one more time, Lord fix me, fix me Lord, please. So I can be right, I don't want to be a hypocrite, I want to be for real, hallelujah, I want to shout for real. I don't want the piano and the organ to shout for me, I want to shout for myself praise the Lord, thank You Jesus. I want to rejoice in my soul, in my mind I want to rejoice. I want you to hold the tambourines, hold the guitars, hold the string instruments, and just let me and my God get together. Peace in my Lord, and you know when you and God get together you got joy and peace. It's not a quiet joy, it's not a testimony joy, it's not a tambourine joy, it's not an emotional thing that everybody is doing. It's just you and the Lord, King David said, that's the joy I want and is looking for. David said, he cried and He heard my cry, I mourned and He heard my mourned, I groaned and He heard my groan.

He came down upon the wings of the morning and God took me by the hands and lifted me out of a horrible pit and He sat me on a rock. When He sat me on a rock, He said, now you can praise the Lord. When David started praising the Lord he got happy and happier and happier. If you want to stay happy you gonna have to praise God in the morning, praise Him in the noonday, praise Him when the sun is going down, praise Him at the breakfast table, praise Him at the dinner table. praise Him on the subway, praise Him on the bus or in the car. Praise Him in tribulation, praise Him in distress, praise Him when nobody likes it, praise Him, praise Him, hallelujah, hallelujah, thank You Jesus.

DEDICATED TO BISHOP WILLIAM L. BONNER

THE CONCRETE JUNGLE

Years ago, in a small town call Greenville SC, beginning in the year of 1966, I was eight years old living in the projects, which were called the concrete jungle. But it's original name was called Fieldcrest and now at this present time is known as Jesse Jackson townhouses. Like any other project a lot went on in it. Some days we played so hard and had so much fun, it felt like a dream. And other days it was like a nightmare with some of the families getting so angry with each other that it became family fights, families fighting families. They would literally, try to kill each other with baseball bats, knives and chains. But fortunately, no one got killed, maybe hurt up but not killed.

I remembered when my best friend Mike would call me at my bedroom window to come out for the night, between the hours of ten and eleven. I would make my bed up like I was in there sleep and slip out my bedroom window, which was two stories high. But as I used to climb out my window, the back porch roof was there for me to land on. And once I got to the ground, Mike was there waiting on me, then the adventure was on. Mike was nine years old, just one year older than me, we both hung out until twelve scoping out the concrete jungle. We were peeping in windows and doors for girls and whatever else we could see. But fortunately, we only seen people with bands, rehearsing for the big times. We also went to the night time softball games to see the girls or boys playing, whom were much older than us.

It was exciting being out in the night, but just like the excitement it was also horror. It was some horrible things we ran into, like for instance, certain guys fighting every other night, I mean tough fighting. Two guys scared me so bad, I didn't come out for a long while. One of the guys had one arm dangling from his shoulder, where you could see the bone and blood running everywhere. While the other guy was beating him with a baseball bat. It was a terrible sight, the worst I've ever seen. So for a while, I watched out my window on the nights they're be fighting repeatedly. It was like a television show, I even learned one of the guys name which was Hambone, after listening to the explicit language and profanity they were using, I would go to bed terrified. But I constantly watched with great wonder of what would happen next.

2

My best friend Mike was a lot tougher than me, maybe because he had older brothers and I didn't. I had four sisters and no brothers. I was in the middle, two older and two younger. But nevertheless, I had to get tougher also, because the other boys would have beef with Mike and take it out on me, because they dare not mess with him. So I had to protect myself and keep a reputation, if not they would call you a punk. You had to stand your grounds in the concrete jungle even if you knew it was a losing battle. Everyday was a challenge, you didn't come out your door without some kind of a challenge.

The most wonderful thing I loved about the concrete jungle was the playground. It seemed like it was in everybody's back door. We did everything in this playground, from playing baseball to playing softball, I mean like we were professionals. We took the games very seriously, so serious we scheduled practices amongst ourselves to play other kids. We played football, basketball and we even played football with car tires, let me explain. Back then, there were scrap tires laying around everywhere, so we would make up games out of almost anything. It wasn't a boring day went by without us doing something. When we played football with the tires, there were about ten or fifteen boys with tires on one team and the same on the other. And we would put the football inside the tire to be tackled and we actually guarded the tire with the football with the other tires, like real football, it was so much fun.

We would have bike racing around the playground. We would plan a date to race and clear everybody off the playground for the event. On every occasion that we had these big events, everyone would be cooperative and whoever that wasn't in the event would be a spectator, someone who cheered us on. In the bike racing it would be about thirty or forty bikes involved. And just like everything else we took it very seriously. If you got bumped over or crashed you was out of the race. I use to love it, I thought I had the fastest bike, even though, I never won. In this playground, which was our backyard had everything in it and everybody from the concrete jungle was there, even from surrounding neighborhoods. We had swings, monkey bars, basketball goals made from scratch, with a wooden backboard and an old bicycle tire rim. We had big marble tournament matches, played hot scotch, four man square and that's why I said before, there wasn't a boring day that went by.

But being in the projects had its ups and downs. I really thanked God for giving us good parents. They were raised in the church and that helped out a lot, because we went occasionally. They wasn't perfect, but they raised us good. People would tell my parents we were very mannerable. My parents used to go out and party with some of the other people in the projects and they would let our grandmother, who also stayed there in the projects, keep us. We really loved her and loved to go to her house because she would let us do a lot of things our parents wouldn't, even though our grandfather was so strict. My grandmother was a very good lady, she had only one problem and that was alcohol, which seemed to consume every adult in the projects. It was the project's worst enemy, even the teenagers would get there hands on it and call their selves sneaking a drink, and as of today, most of them are alcoholics. The older guys would get wine or liquor and pass it down to us younger guys to drink. I would take a few swallows, but as time went on I really turned against it. After seeing the older guys taking advantage of the old drunk men, going through their pockets taking their money in order to get themselves a drink. And knowing that my father and grandmother and uncles had established bad drinking problems, I moved further and further away from it. I thanked God though, that the older guys didn't ever harm my people. They used to come and get me when my father and grandmother would be laying somewhere drunk. I remember one time the guys came and told me my grandmother was laying out in the grass in front of her apartment. I came up to her thinking she was knocked out, saying grandma, grandma get up and as I went to touch her, she swung at me and looked at me saying, "Earlyboy is that you". I said, yes grandma it's me, let me take you in the house, I was only eight years old at the time. She reached up and pulled up on me and once she got up she twisted my ear, which she did all the time when she was drunk. Everytime she twisted my ear it hurt so bad, but I loved her so much, and we went on in the house.

Now times was moving on and I was getting older. My eyes were noticing things, I didn't really like. The people in the neighborhood were making me irritated, coming in and out of your apartment, borrowing sugar, flour and whatever else it was to borrow. Catching you in your night clothes or even your underwear. What mostly upsetted me was when we used to go to the musical hop in the park across town in another black neighborhood and getting run out because of fights amongst the older guys. They would fight each other into a bloody mess, just because they were from different parts of town. It was disgusting, because at this time Martin Luther King was marching for our rights and they were fighting because they were from different territories.

One day my mother and I was going to the City Hall and we got on the bus and went all the way to the back, regardless of empty seats to the front. Then once we arrived at the City Hall, it was a hot summer day and while waiting in line, I got thirsty. So I ran to the water fountain and started to drink and my mother stopped me. She made me notice the sign on the wall, which quoted, "whites only", and she told me, I couldn't drink out of it. Now, I was beginning to see things differently, my thoughts and feelings had started getting real serious about life. The things that bothered me in our black cultural ways were bothering me even more. The beating of three black guys in our neighborhood because they were at a girl's party and someone found out they were from across town. They beat them and ran them out of the neighborhood. After seeing how the whites were living and comparing to how the blacks were living I got deeply depressed. The obnoxious thing about it was that I didn't get mad at the whites as much as I did the blacks. Because it depressed me to see us destroy ourselves fighting each other instead of trying to come together and build. From day to day, from time to time, I would isolate myself from everybody and get in my favorite rocking chair in the middle of the room and rock myself to sleep. But before I would go to sleep, I would think about my future from the projects. Out of my despair of being an eight year old kid, It was times when I said, I will make a whole lot of money and buy up everything worth buying and owning every business I can own. I wanted to gain so much power that I'd be recognized in the white collar world. I had said to myself, "one day I'm going to owned so much that I was going to change Greenville to Earlville".

So I would sit in my rocking chair all the day long concentrating on how I could get out of the projects and start my quest toward success, while my sisters would be out playing and enjoying life. My father would come and asked me what was wrong with me and I would tell him, "nothing I'm alright." I would hear him in their room telling my mother that it was something wrong with him. He is not like his sisters, he just sits in that rocking chair all day. He acts like he's retarded or losing his mind.

But as time went on, I came out of my depression and got with the program of playing with my friends. But I still stayed focus on what was going on around me and was taking life more seriously. Integrating was taking form and things was really beginning to change at school and at home. Things was actually getting better, my parents was getting financially better and more stable in their marriage. They even bought a house in the month of February 1972. I was thirteen going on fourteen, when my sisters and I was experiencing a whole new atmosphere from the concrete jungle to a big house in a predominate white neighborhood. It wasn't easy, we would walk to the stores or around the neighborhood trying to get familiar with the place and white people would hollow out their car windows "niggers" and throw bottles or cans at us. They would break bottles and throw trash in front of the house even in our yard. I remembered our first day going to the bus stop meeting white kids face to face, they were nice though. One of the guys became a close friend of mine. But what got me the most was that everyday we came home from school, while walking along the way, some white kids in diapers would be in their yard yelling "niggers" and they couldn't even go to the bathroom on their own, I couldn't understand it at the time. So I asked my mother, why was kids, that young calling us niggers. I was thinking they were to young to even know anything about the word "nigger". But my mom explained it to me, she said, they didn't know any better, they were just copying the words of their parents. And she said, just look over it.

Regardless of the change, it was time to get busy, so I went out and found my first job as a paperboy. From there each job was getting better and better. My mind was staying more occupied on work and making money, so I could avoid thinking of the good times we had in the concrete jungle with our friends. I went back a few times and finally, I gave it up and began adapting to the new neighborhood. One day my father got me a job working in a mattress company. Little to my knowledge, my first day, I noticed over half of the guys there were from the concrete jungle. I was amazed and so happy to see my friends again. The most enjoyable thing about it was that my best friend Mike was there and we jumped with joy. We had so much fun there, everyday was a good day. One day, Mike seen that I was riding my bike to work so he wanted to reunite with me. So he told me, he would pulled his bike out of storage and meet me half way so we could ride together. As I was riding my bike home that day, I couldn't help for thinking that we were going to get our brotherly love back again. I told my sisters, Mike and I had come back together again. I was so happy I went to bed with a smile on my face.

The next morning when I awaken, I jumped up quickly and got ready, got my bike and went to the place we were to meet. When I seen that he wasn't there, I assumed he had forgot or he had problems with his bike. Then, I thought he could had rode with his friends. So I came on to work and after preparing myself for work, I came out the locker room looking for Mike, to see what happen. After I didn't see him or his brothers, I asked someone where are they. This guy told me, Mike was in an accident on his bike with his girlfriend. I asked what happen and he said, as they were riding down this hill together with her on the back, a drunk driver came up behind them and knock them in the air. And when Mike came back down his head hit the windshield. Then I asked are they alive, he said the girl lived but Mike died. My lips dropped down in my chest, my eyes got watery and I ran out that place, got on my bike and cried all the way home. I was in a state of shock and all I could think of was, it was my fault. I thought, if he wouldn't have pulled his bike out, which he had put up for some years, he would be still alive. But because of me he died, I couldn't get it off of my mind. I asked God why did this had to happen? He wasn't that bad, he mostly defended himself in that rough place, he was really good. I just couldn't understand, how two people were so happy from not seeing each other for a long time, end so drastic, I blamed myself for years. Time past and I started hanging on the opposite side of town where my cousins lived, searching for that brotherly love again. But one thing I finally learned as I kept on living was that brotherly love was hard to come by because you don't receive it like you give it, especially when you already have a bunch of brothers around you all the time. My closest brother was Mike who gave himself better than anyone I've ever seen. Fortunately, life goes on and later in life I finally found someone better and closer than a brother, Jesus.

I was working a full time job, from 4-12 while in the ninth grade. My parents would complain and even my coach at school, about me working so many hours. My coach would asked me, want you come out and play ball for me? Then he said, you have all your life to work. But I was thinking about the dollar bill and improving my status. Nevertheless, I continued to keep my grades up around A&B average, I was persistent on being something in life. But as I headed toward the eleventh and twelfth grades I had started slipping in my grades from A&B average to C&D average. All because I was hanging out with guys smoking marijuana. I remember I used to go to class so high that I couldn't function. Most of the teachers knew me as being a smart young fellow, but they begun to see the slackness in my work. They constantly told me, I was failing in my classes. In my senior year the teachers told me if I didn't straighten up, I wasn't going to make it. So I got to thinking, this will keep me from moving on to my destiny. So I stop hanging out with the "potheads" and got to some serious business with my school work. I barely past that year with a D average. I did graduate with my class and received my diploma. But emptying myself from wanting anymore schooling, including college. From the rocking chair to the end of high school was a growing experience.

I am so glad our parents took us to church. We may not have went every Sunday, but we went enough to know what it was all about. We even got baptize voluntarily one by one. It was the funniest thing though, I was about twelve and I had two sisters older and two younger and I was in the middle, we followed one another, Sunday to Sunday until all was baptize. We had discussed who would go next, and we had to encourage one another, because we all were scared. At the time, we were told by our parents that at twelve years old we were responsible for ourselves in coming to the Lord so we got baptize. I sure thanked God my parents took us to church and I think all parents should do so. Just like the Bible say, "train up a child in the way he or she should go, and when he is old he will not depart from them". I encourage this scripture, especially now.

I had started working at an early age, being a paperboy at thirteen and working at a restaurant at the age of fourteen and fifteen. And moving on to a full time job, while in high school. So once I graduated from high school I was so use to working, I wanted to continue working, instead of going to college or the military. So during my last year of high school a friend told me about this new career job that just landed in town. He told me to hurry and put in my application and I done just that. They hired me the same month I graduated. It was one of the highest paying jobs in town, and my future was just beginning. Now that first year, I went and bought a brand new car, after begging my father to co-sign. From a small boy in a little rocking chair in the middle of the room until now, I was beginning to have a change of thoughts. Life was staring me in the face now, and the challenge was demanding. So demanding, that I was trying to be an adult before I knew how. I was being disrespectful and disobedient to my parents under their roof. To the point, where I would try to fight my parents back, wanting to be grown.

Well guess what, after my last and crucial fight with my father, I moved out to my own apartment. Now it was time to be grown, and let me tell you it wasn't easy. One advise, don't never leave home on a bad note. That's the worst thing you can do. I landed an apartment right in the middle of another predominate white neighborhood. Imagine me nineteen years old, a new car, and my dog, I had the furniture company deliver me three rooms of furniture, a kitchen set, a living room set, and a bedroom set all at one delivery, not knowing I was being watched. Nevertheless, through all the excitement of having my own apartment, I started putting everything in place. I even appointed my dog his own room with his eating bowl and a rug. By the way, whose name was Duke, in which we were like soulmates, he was my best friend. We really kicked it together, especially now during our first time away from home. We became closer and closer, to the point that I was talking to him like he was a human. So I told Duke it's time to get a stereo system for some entertainment. I didn't have a television, because I wasn't into watching to much television. I went out and bought a stereo system with the biggest speakers I've ever seen. Now things were beginning to unravel. Nineteen years old with one of the highest paid jobs in Greenville, and driving a brand new car with a two bedroom apartment full of furniture and a brand new stereo, it was party time. Little that I knew, that everyone in the neighborhood were watching me. But nevertheless, it was on, I would invite people over everytime I was off work. At times,when I had to go to work, I would only get just two hours of sleep.

My next door neighbor would constantly knock on the wall, for me to turn down the music. It had gotten where, I would get kind of upset at them for constantly knocking on the wall. But after I seen they had a little child, I would really be considerate of that, and keep down the music. My girlfriend from high school would come over occasionally to check on me and clean and cook for me. She complained about me partying to much. I was living the life, having card games, inviting girls over for drinks and letting so-called friends come with their girls to handle their business. See my girlfriend couldn't come over unless I went and got her, so I thought. So I done pretty much what I wanted to do until my girlfriend busted me one night and turned it out.

As time went on, I wasn't indulging only in alcohol but I had started back indulging in marijuana also. And me and some friends of mind would smoke until sometimes we would past out. It had gotten to the point, where I was getting behind on my bills. Even though, I had a good paying job, I had started neglecting my responsibilities, by partying to much. Depression was beginning to set in, I was getting worst instead of better. Other matters didn't get any better either. One day I went to work at 3pm and didn't get home until 12:00 am. When I pulled up in the driveway, I automatically went toward the backyard to check on Duke, whom I kept chained up while I was at work. In which at this time I thought was a good idea, because he would have the apartment in a mess when I got home. But unfortunately, it wasn't the same, because the closer I got to him the more I heard him mourning and whining. As I wondered why, I seen where he had been cut wide open from one side of his back to the other side. I was highly upset, not knowing what to do. I knelt down to him crying, wondering what in the world happen to you. Then I took him in the house and wrapped a towel around him to stop the bleeding. I couldn't sleep all night for thinking who could have done such a thing. Thoughts aroused my suspicion of trying to figure out, if it was my next door neighbor or someone else in the neighborhood. I was surrounded by prejudice, but I never paid it no mind. So I said to myself, the guy next door shouldn't had a reason because I started cooperating with the music. I was compelled to asked my neighbor what happen or did he hear anything, but just like I thought, he denied hearing or seeing anything. I got up the next morning and took Duke to the veterinarian. They put in eighty-nine stitches and a bucket over his head to keep him from taking the stitches out. Everyday I would come in and nurse Duke and feel sorry for him having to wear that bucket on his head.

One early bright sunny day, a friend and I was in the front yard washing our cars, laughing and joking. And here comes this old half gray and half blonde white man, drunk and staggering into the yard. He gave a comment about the loud music we were playing. Might of fact, his exact words were, "y'all young boys with that loud music, y'all be playing all the time is going to stop. Then he said, that dog you have back there barking, is going to stop too. When he mentioned about my dog, I immediately questioned him about the incident. Then he answered indirectly saying, someone needs to shoot him. My anger was beginning to arise, so I demanded the man to leave out my yard. At this time, I was glad I wasn't a violent man. I spoke to my father about the situation and he brought up how I left home and moved without any advice from him. On top of that, he said, "moving in that predominate white neighborhood by yourself not knowing anything about being on your own", was crazy anyway. But through all the chastisement, he finally said, let it go, but I wanted to call the police or take matters in my own hands. But my Pops just said move out from over there.

So like I was saying before one problem led to another, now my girlfriend pops up pregnant and crying about her father was going to put her out when he find out. My dog nearly gets murdered and I was behind on all my bills because of poor management, I was about to go nuts. I cried and prayed asking myself and God, what am I going to do. I looked at my situation and thought, if I would had only stayed home a little longer, I wouldn't have been in this mess. The mere thought of me going back home was stunning, with my dad standing at the front door with a iron fist. I took a deep breath, stood back on my heels, and said, "I'm out here now so I have to take it like a man".

Waking up the next morning with a bright sunny day staring me in the face, excited me very much, until I was back thinking of my situation again. My girlfriend would constantly asked me, what are we going to do? The pressure was on and backing me against the wall. I felt so alone, even though I wasn't, I didn't know which way to turn, I knew I didn't want to go home, because of the heat. I really needed advice, being young and out on my own for the very first time, was more serious than I thought. But with me being stubborn, I continued to struggle and party at the same time. I guess what you call laughing and crying at the same time. I had some sleepless nights, some worrying and crying and sometimes listening to music until I fell asleep, with Duke sleeping at the foot of the bed. My girlfriend didn't let up, she continued to remind me of her predicament, what it really boiled down to was that she wanted to move in with me. But the only way her father could let her go was through marriage. So she done the most brilliant thing I've ever seen. She got her best friend to come over to my house early one morning, rushing me to get ready and come with her. I got up in a daze, got myself together and proceeded with her and her friend, whom I knew real well.

We ended up at the courthouse, and we rushed right in while her friend parked the car. Now, I couldn't figure out what was going on, I was just in the middle. Finally a Judge showed up as if he knew what was going on. Then he pops out the vows and I said wait we don't have a witness. Forgetting about her friend, who came through the door as I was speaking. So here I was married before I could even think about it. The very next morning I couldn't believe it, I thought it was a dream. This was a start of a new beginning, from the sleepless nights and the crying and talking to God. In return, He gives me a new life of marriage.

THE NEW LIFE OF MARRIAGE

So now here we are married, and my wife pregnant with our first baby, and now we're in the midst of trying to figure out how to break the news to her father. Sleeping in two different houses when you're married was kind of ridiculous. Since I was the man, I took it on my shoulders to tell her father. He was a serious man, and for strictly business. Doing this behind his back was really out of character, so someone had to break the news. I knew she wasn't, because she had already been complaining about her daddy using her like she was a maid. But you see, her mother had an operation in her head for a tumor cancer, which was a successful operation, except leaving her three quarter blind. Therefore she couldn't do a lot around the house, which left my wife very dependent upon. She done everything around the house from cleaning to cooking. Now you see why it was so difficult to tell her father, but nevertheless, I stood up to the challenge. One good thing about it, him and I were really good friends. One thing I did know, always try to win the father over first. So I spoke to him about it and it wasn't as hard as I thought. He simply okayed it and started planning for my future with her. As she was beginning to move in with me in my apartment, her father came over for the first time by his self and looked things over. He suggested an idea to me that I've never thought of. He mentioned about moving in with him to save money for ourselves. At the time, I was kind of in a bind and needed rescuing. This sounded like the best solution to my problem, so I took advantage of the opportunity and said yes. Now my wife didn't know what was going on. When I presented it to her, she was totally against it. She told me, it was just a way for her father to keep her as a maid. But my mind was made up, so I talked her into going along with me.

I sold all my furniture and moved the rest of my stuff in with her family. Let me tell you, it was totally different than what I was use to. Here I was, in the middle of a family with different ways from my family. I had already been adjusting and adapting to different situations, so I had to learn their ways also, and make some changes within myself. Her father took me under his wing and taught me the means of survival, the reality of staying alive in this forsaken world. He made it real serious about taking care of your family, if it cause you your life. He was mainly taken over, where I didn't allow my father to do. Everyday was a lesson and we spent more time together than I did with my wife. Even though, my father-in-law constantly drilled in me the seriousness of making money and building a foundation for my family, I would still do the things a twenty year old would do. Like waste my time with the fellows and smoke weed and even try to sell some, when I didn't have to because I had one of the best jobs in town. But being in the hood, I thought that would make the fellows look up to me, and it did. Like I said before, my father-in-law was a serious man and he always spoke on success. He owned his own moving company, owned a store and ran other side businesses. If he would have known I was slowly moving in the marijuana business, he would've been highly upset and probably kicked me out of his house. Even though, I longed to have my own business too. I even made attempts on trying, by meeting big business men and discussing the cost of rent on their buildings. They would look at me and asked me what kind of back up do you have. They would say, you are so young, and I would play it off like I had some powerful backup but they seen right through me. So I continued helping my father-in-law in his store and other things, and fall right back doing my ghetto hustling.

Now it was December, 1978, finally my wife had our first baby, she was a doll. She had a head full of curly hair and Chinese eyes and a light tan. She was beautiful and everybody loved her. So now, it was three of us and we had to make arrangements for our own place. We still remained a little longer until the baby started aggravating my wife's father more and more. My wife was also getting aggravated and putting more pressure on me to move. I went out searching for somewhere to stay and I found a cheap little apartment. I showed it to my wife and she said she'll take anything to get out of the house. I went on and put a down payment on the apartment, we started painting the inside with some beautiful colors. Then, when her father heard about us moving, he step in with another solution, which totally went against my wife plans. She even tried to tell me not to listen to her father, telling me he was just trying to keep her under him, then saying, "he hates losing me". Which I knew she was probably right, but I couldn't help for just listening to what he had to say. He came to me as a business man like before and counting myself as a business man, I had to see what was on his mind. And sure enough, he had an exceptionally great plan, one I couldn't refuse. It made me convince my wife to try it one more time.

So we ended up canceling the apartment and going along with the plan. Oh yeah, this was the plan, if we came back in to live with him, we could claim a separate residence. He had heard and found information about a highway was coming through his property and they would give anyone living there money to get another place. Little that we knew, God was blessing us with our first house with no money out of our pockets. It's amazing when God recognizes us, when we don't even recognize ourselves or God. I sit back now and shed tears on how we ignored God and acted like He didn't exist. But out of His patience, grace and longsufferings, He still loves and have mercy on us. This is the reason why we have to praise Him.

The plan came through and the highway paid my father-in-law house off and gave him enough to almost pay off another house and they gave us two thousand to put down on a house. Still, my wife wanted to get farthest away from her father as possible, but he was persistent for us to live close to each other. For what he done for us, I went along with him. We searched high and low for two houses in the same neighborhood. Finally, we found two houses across the street from each other. At this time, our first child was a year old and my wife was already seven months pregnant with the second one. Everything was falling in place right on time as if God was planning every move, which He was, we just couldn't see it. We closed the deal without paying any closing cost and moved on in, with my father-in-law not far behind us. It was a beautiful thing, a dream come true, being in our very first place together. Being patient and listening to her father, really paid off. Regardless of her pulling against it, we prevailed and hung in there. God blesses us even when we don't notice. He continues to bless us hoping that we will see His goodness. Once we got settled in, we got acquainted right away with the neighbors. They were the kind of neighbors that came to us and made themselves known.

A few years had went by and we had two little girls now and one on the way, it seemed like we fell in a glove that fitted just right. Early one bright sunny morning my door bell was ringing off the wall. I thought, who in the world could this be early in the morning, except her dad. So I got up to see who it was, and sure enough it was my father-in-law at the door calling me doctor, doctor once a doctor always a doctor. He always called me doctor or mate, which was what everybody called him. Anyway, he told me, let's get up and get these yards together. I told my wife this was going to be a problem. I think I had just made the biggest mistake of my life, moving across the street from your father-in-law. And for sure, he kept me on the ball, he became more and more of a mentor to me though. It had it's advantages, because I was being taught a lot of things from him. And from his teachings, I could tell he must have had a rough life, and now he was willing to teach another, not to fall in those same mistakes, even though, some were predestined to happen. But he kept me sharp and I appreciated it and I took it in, very well. But still, living across the street from him had it's disadvantages also, because he would worry me at the most inopportune time, which aggravated me so much.

But other than that, my family were growing, my wife was having babies right behind each other. So I told her, I would take care all the bills until the kids was in school. I was still working in the same place, I had started after high school. This was a job, where I was glad to go to work. We worked on production, but regardless, we had a lot of fun, and with me being one of the youngest, I kept some of the older people with excitement everyday. We had became a close family on all shifts. It wouldn't be any strangers, everybody was welcome. Then one day, I met this white guy working in the administration building by himself wearing overalls, cleaning offices. I got acquainted with him as I was getting copies made each day for my job. We would talk about our families and surprisely one day he asked me was I Saved. I told him, I was baptize when I was twelve. He told me it wasn't the same thing, then he explained to me, what was being Saved all about. I listened patiently and that night I accepted the Lord Jesus Christ. After this acceptance, I've never seen this man again.

I carried on with life with the best job a man could asked for and the best little family anyone could think of. I would give my wife most of the money to pay the bills. We had a good system going on until a phone call came up and it was a bill collector calling about not being paid in three months. I told them that was impossible, because my wife paid everything. But more calls came in from other bill collectors, even the house was three months behind. I questioned her and she told me she got carried away at the Mall. As to this day, I couldn't understand why she done such a thing. So I started dedicating most of my time at work, trying to grab all the overtime I could, so I could get caught up again. I couldn't stand it, living behind so I worked sixteen hours a day until I was more than caught up. I paid everything off and told my wife, now if we need anything, we can pay cash for it. The only payments we had was the house payment and the utility bills.

Now, our third little girl was born and she was a doll also. And on her second year of age my father-in-law, her grandfather, my teacher or mentor got very sick and died. Leaving behind in the house, his wife who was three quarters blind and his youngest daughter who was slightly retarded. With his death, it brought on a change with our family, also. My wife and I was drawing away from each other for some reason or another. Most of the time my wife and children would be staying across the street and after I got off from work I would stay home alone. I tried to understand, my wife wanted to be there for their protection. The more time went on, I would start hanging out after work with the fellows at the clubs and all night spots. Slowly I was drifting back into selling weed. Little that I knew, the wheels was getting ready to run off since my "mentor" had died.

One night, when I came in and my wife had been cut across the face. I had to rush her to the hospital and they stitched her up and said, she was lucky it didn't hit her across her temple. She explained to me, her older sister boyfriend was mad at her and mistakenly got her mixed up with her sister. So I rested on that statement and wanted to go and do something about it, but she told me not to worry about it, just let it go. I just couldn't understand why she wanted to drop it, but I normally done as I was told. Later in time past, I heard a totally different story than what was told to me that night. Even though, at that time we were separated already, I was still very much upset. The story was that she was slipping around on me and cheated someone out of some money and they came back for revenge. But at that time, I believed her story so we continued in agreement, with her staying with her mother awhile and staying with me awhile. I tried to understand her obligations, but on the otherhand, I was hanging out more and more. I even had started a relationship with this lady, it lasted a little while until we finally cut it off. My wife was evidently up for suspicion, because she was disrespecting me by talking to guys romantically, right in my face. Regardless, I got more and more into the marijuana business. The money was beginning to look good and I was spending more of my time being a salesman than being a husband.

I was beginning to think about the time when I used to sit in that rockingchair in the middle of my room, how I dreamed of taking over Greenville. So now, I was beginning to get busy buying and selling marijuana locally. Things were getting in high demands, I started recruiting people to work with me. One of the guys, I recruited became a close friend and his name was Calvin. Calvin was mostly a consumer and all he wanted to do was consumed, otherwords, smoke marijuana. But I put it in his head, to be a producer instead of a consumer. He became a very good producer, even though he liked consuming also. We were getting bigger and we needed to branch out so we connected up with a guy out of town in a little place called Orangeburgh. It was about one hundred miles away.

Might of fact, I lost my first two thousand dollars getting connected up with this guy. Simply because, we met this runner or small time hustler on the block where they sold drugs. He would take us about one block from the house of a guy that sold quantity in weight and told us to park and stay there, because the guy didn't want to meet any new guys. So we took a chance a number of times dealing with this small time hustler and he came through each time. Until one night, he had us parked a little farther from the house. We waited and waited, I started complaining about the time, but Calvin said, don't worry boss, he hadn't let us down, so far. I waited until I couldn't wait any longer. We approached the house and didn't see a sign of the small time guy. We knocked on the door and explained to the guy who we were, and what we had been doing through this guy. He told us he never seen him on this night, then he said he think the guy was getting on "crack", which we knew nothing about because it was just coming out. We jumped in the car and went searching for him in some places we knew he hung out at, with our guns in our hands, going around people we didn't know, asking have they seen him. But still, we came up empty, so we counted that as a lost, but we ended up meeting our connection face to face. In spite of the loss, we gained tremendously, working directly with this guy. We grew and made trips quite often until he started getting slack with his business and it was getting harder and harder to reach him. Sometimes he would be in the house and wouldn't open the door. I came to a conclusion that he must have gotten on that drug called "crack" also. Before leaving that town, some of the guys told us, he had loss it, meaning the drug had taken him over. So after hearing this I stop going down there.

GETTING DEEP IN THE GAME

My partner and I were big timers now, our clientele had grew and the demands were getting higher. Even though, I loved my three little girls and my wife and dog, "Duke", I was moving in the fastlane with excitement and the money was making me hop on every occasion. One thing I did do while on the road, I constantly bought my family back gifts. But little that I knew, I was drifting away more and more from my family. My closest daughter was drawing farther and farther from me and I was to blind to see it. I just kept on taking care of business after the Orangeburgh trip ceased. I had to come up with a connection real quick and fortunately, I did. A local fellow who stayed about twenty minutes from me. So we got busy on the bandwagon with this guy. I was buying army duffer bags full of marijuana. I was getting him paid as well as myself, and we became close buddies during these transactions. I even started up a new business from the money I was making off this guy. It was a record and tape music store, which done pretty good for a while, until the economy got bad and things slowed down considerably, so I closed the store down. I continued hustling with the local guy, who was supplying me dearly with all the marijuana, I needed. Then all of a sudden, he started slacking off too. His ability to keep up was slowing down, he was also going under with the cocaine and crack effectiveness. Finally, this connection came to a halt also and I was still in high demands. I had begun to worry about this business more than my job. I remind you, I still had one of the best jobs in town. But my focus was going into the weed business because of the money and the fun.

A cousin of mine, who was staying in Detroit had come back home and started hanging out with me. He schooled me in on some connections in Miami, Florida. We started making trips to Florida, which was totally new to me and it really hyped me up. We landed at a house called the drop-off, we stayed there until pickups were made. There were older women staying there, who we called old school hustlers. One of them, I had found a liken to, real quick, she was the one who made connections for us, she was gorgeous and quick on her feet. Elaine was her name, and she first started taking us in a little Spanish town called Lil Havana. After a few times there, we got real acquainted with the Cubans, we were warned not to deal with the Colombians, because they were dangerous and heartless. One day, while she had us at a poolroom, the funniest thing happen while we all were sitting around eating chicken feet, which after I found out what it was I wouldn't eat anymore. But anyway, I rode off with a Cuban, without anyone knowing. He was trying to hook me up with some guy at a nightclub and the first thing they asked me, was I Jamaican, I said no why, then they told me the Jamaicans were known to rob Cubans. Then I asked were they Colombians, they said no. We laughed about it, but I had a desperate feeling that I needed to get back. We drove back to the poolroom where everybody were and Elaine was terrified because I ran off by myself. She told me don't never do that again, you are in Miami, they will kill you down here. Joking with her, I pulled out my little 25 automated pistol and started to shoot in the air, bragging to her that it would've been a shootout if they would've started anything, but the gun jammed on me. I was surprised and upset, while laughing it off, but knowing the seriousness of what she was saying.

One of the incidents, occurred one night when one of our connections had gotten on drugs and decided he wanted to rob us. He tried every means to rob me but I asked him, are you trying to rob me and he broke down and told me yes, go home Earl you are a good person. Between this incident and the few incidents I had in New York, I'm very sure now that God was with me. The more trips we made, the more she took us to more and more connections. We went as far as Keywest to get loaded up with weed. As soon as we got back to town we would sell everything, and at times I would turn around to go back to get more. Now, my cousin was on the payroll along with a couple more guys including my first partner and friend, Calvin.

My job was getting in jeopardy, because of the trips, plus my family were getting into jeopardy also. My Supervisor had put me on the last warning, he wanted to fire me so bad. And because of this I would slow down and live a family man life and hang around the house a little more. In doing so, I was noticing how my wife was seemingly slipping around, acting like she wasn't caring anymore. I tried to overlook her because when I questioned her, she would shoot me a line like, don't worry about me, you haven't been worrying about me before. I just kept concentrating on the business, my job, and maintaining the household. I had really became a full pledge gansta. I hung out at the clubs with my crew showing everybody that I was one of the big dawgs. I carried pistols everywhere I went, I took the game real seriously.

One day, I came home and Duke had gotten hit by a car and was shaking like he had gone into a coma. Being upset as I was, I just stood there not knowing what to do. Calvin and I picked him up, carried him in the yard, while still stunned I pulled out my 45 special pistol and was compelled to put him out his misery. Then I shot him five times in the head, telling Calvin we'll bury him tomorrow, let's go get a drink at the club. This was done at five o'clock PM, when I came back home around twelve AM, I was pretty toasted. I staggered in the back yard to check Duke out, just to found out that he was still breathing after five shots to the head. I broke down with guilt, wondering if he could have lived if I've taken him to the doctor. I cried all night and carried it on my shoulders for a long time. The next morning he was dead, Calvin and I buried him about six feet deep. Still I was feeling a deep remorse for how I handled Duke situation, which caused me to asked myself what kind of man have I became? Nevertheless, the hustling game was getting stronger and stronger. I even told my crew don't ever let anyone come between the business, especially a woman. We road hard and long, up and down the east coast hauling marijuana like it was bootleg alcohol. Seeing my family, but losing them. I would bring my girls gifts when I came back home, but little did I know, I was destroying the hearts of my daughters, especially the one I favored the most.

Times were moving on, and things were changing, the law was getting more strict and hard on the marijuana business, so we had to get wiser. We changed our tactics, we started working with beepers and using phones. Let me remind you, I was a Saved man by announcement, but didn't understand a thing about it. All I knew was, I believed there was a God and I believed Jesus rose from the dead. Matter of fact, it never crossed my mind again, if I could recollect. I was getting ready to enter into another era or realm of my life without realizing it. The marijuana business was seizing and was getting real scarce. After making a trip down Florida and not being able to find any weed, I was highly disappointed. My cousin who was part of the crew, and who had came from Detroit because his mob boss had gotten killed, so he came back fearing for his life, made a suggestion to me about moving in the cocaine business. He and another associate who was also part of the crew were together in Detroit. They were full bloomed in the cocaine business. they were so involved, in their own spare time they would be free basing, a form of getting high off the product. While being in disappointment with the long trips from coming up empty handed, it wasn't hard to be convinced of another way. But this wasn't the first time he tried to get me to get in the cocaine business, I would just ignore him. But now I was kind of desperate, so I let him convince me in making a move, knowing I didn't know a thing about the business but he was there to coach me.

Now the movie "Scarface" was just coming out and it helped promote the product and gave me a higher incentive to sell. We made some positive connections with this new product and made a big score on a deal. Our first trip back in town, we had to get out on the streets to make contacts to push or promote this new product. I have to tell you, this stuff put me in a whole different status. I was making contact with people I use to buy from, but now selling to. An older guy explained to me, in this business who you buy from you also can sell to. So we got busy selling and moving the product real well. It gave me a new sense of nervousness. I also realized how I was jeopardizing my family in the process. So I constantly searched for some weed to sell. At not one time, did I ask myself the question, why even bother to get drugs? Why am I so driven to stay in this game? I had one of the best jobs in town.

Anyway, I continued on until the DEA got involved and begun to investigate. A young guy from the narcotic squad came by my house to warn me, I was being watched. His words were, "I'm a relative of your wife's brother through marriage and I heard of you down at the jailhouse". Guys are getting arrested and bringing up your name, saying how good you are to them by giving them a chance to make money off nothing. The way they were talking about you, I thought you was living like the movie "Scarface", otherwords, a top of the line gangster. I looked him dead in the eye and told him to look around, do I look like I'm doing so well. Even though I was so dirty, with pounds of marijuana in the house, I continued to keep my cool. He finished the conversation by telling me an informer had came to my house and bought some drugs and the task force were coming in sometime this week, but he didn't know when exactly. He asked me for a bag of weed for his service, but secretly I was nervous, so I told him I didn't have anymore. Being surprised by this guy, I have to admit he did have me shook up. Soon after he left the house, I Started immediately, cleaning out the house transporting everything to one of my other cousins, where I secretly took care a lot of business.

Before the week was out, one early sunny morning, my family and I was just finishing up breakfast, when there was a knock at the door! when I looked around, there was a tall guy standing at the door with a pimp hat on. I couldn't recognize who it was because he had his head down. Ohh, but when he raised his head, I instantly knew who he was. I tried to shut the door on him, but his crew came from somewhere and they bogarded their way in. They demanded for us to sit on the sofa, then he asked me to tell where the drugs were or they were going to tear up the house. I told them there were no drugs, so do your job. They searched the whole house, but came up empty, except for a five dollar bag of marijuana I had for myself. They handcuffed me in the presence of my kids, then put me in the back of their jeep and drove me to the station. They fingerprinted me, took my picture, then told me,"I can go. I was puzzled for a while, thinking they were up to something and because of this, I took it easy for a while. I was thinking they would be watching me, but I didn't hear from them no time soon. After this the wheels run off.

One day I came home from work frustrated, seeing my wife and part of my crew sitting around in the living room doing nothing, waiting on me to come in. I told everybody including my wife, "y'all goin miss me, when I leave this place", y'all need to get some business about yourselves and quit waiting on me. I had already been trying to get my wife to do something with her life, since the kids had started school. I had spoke something right there, that was going to turn my life around and I didn't realize it. The crew and I were getting busier, the era was changing, cocaine was taking the streets over and marijuana were phasing out. The trips we were making was becoming more cocaine trips. I would still try to bounce back to the marijuana business, but it was getting impossible. The cocaine business was in and I was learning a good bit about it, not knowing it was leading me toward destruction. I was beginning to think I was invincible. I was telling my crew we were the untouchables. Then here comes the cocaine parties in Fort Lauderdale and Miami. They would try to talk me into giving them drugs to get high on but I would refuse everytime. They wouldn't give up though, they were very persistent in trying to persuade me to give in, I finally gave everybody enough to party with. My cousin from Detroit still wasn't satisfied, he constantly asked me to join them and quit being an odd ball. But I refused them repeatedly, then I told them, what do you all see in that stuff. They would say, come and see and I'll say no thanks. My cousin would even send the girls after me to manipulate me. Then finally, one day I let them convince me to try it. As I sit down at the table where everybody were, when it came to my turn, I gently smoked some and told everybody I didn't feel a thing. They said keep trying it, you'll feel something soon or later. And I done just that, thinking my mind was to strong to let it get me like them, if I only knew! While doing it as a social high and on social occasions, I started dipping and dabbing with it more and more. Then I started bringing it close to home. I would go in a room in the house to try to freebase or get high while everyone were sleep. This cocaine had started pulling me apart without me even noticing it. Was I becoming like the guys I was buying from before, who fell by the wayside?

THE TRICK OF THE ENEMY

My wife and I were beginning to have fights over everything. One day I came home from work and she started accusing me of another woman. She was furious, threatening me to get out, but I ignored her, claiming my innocence. I don't know if somebody were speaking out lies on me or what. All I knew, she took it a step farther by throwing out my clothes in the rain. I told her, this was the third time you've kicked me out of my own house, then I told her this is the last straw, I'm not coming back. I gathered up my clothes off the ground. Then I went over my cousin's house, where I called the secret place. This was where I handled a lot of drug business, but this time I was there to let off stress from being highly disturbed. Because this incident was nowhere in the plans. And while sitting around with my head twisted, I was going around in circles trying to figure out what to do next.

During this time, was the time I met this woman, I called the Mistress, because she was a mysterious woman. She resembled a Creole, she was tall, tan and beautiful. She was from New York and unlike any woman I've ever seen in these parts. I was instantly overtaken by her, I put everything aside for the moment. I went out on a few dates with her and was amazed. By this time my wife was calling for me to come back home. She even staged a birthday party in my absence, inviting family from both sides, plus lots of friends as though nothing had happen. But now, I had got fed up with our situation so I ignored her call and booked a trip with this new mistress. My wife gave the party expecting me to come, but I was one hundred and fifty miles away enjoying the company of the new mistress. After this rendezvous with her, my mind was mesmerized. And the sad thing about it was, I was going blind of the responsibility of my kids. Now I was very confused on what to do, after experiencing the best sensation of my life, so I thought, or going back to my family. The reasonable choice would be going back to my family, in which I did. I went back but it wasn't the same anymore because I had an added attraction. I started letting the mistress take drug runs with me and the crew. We were slipping around with each other so much that I went and got another house just for her and I. Things were going so fast, it was like someone else was planning my life for me, without my permission.

My wife and I were having fights over this situation and she was trying hard to keep this marriage together, now that it had got to this point. It was on the verge of a departure, I was willing to give up my marriage for an illusion. My wife was really making it rough for me, I mean she was applying on the pressure. It got harder and harder trying to run two houses, working on a job and hustling too. So I left my good paying job to go full-time in the drug game, in order to have more freedom.

Things were getting kind of hectic but regardless, I kept on pushing like a blind man through the woods, not knowing which way to go and not knowing how to stop the madness. My crew were getting upset over this move I was making with this mistress. Simply because we had made an oath of not letting nothing or anybody come between us and the business. And I was the first to break the oath. My cousin, the one who introduced me to cocaine was now having financial problems and was coming to me for help. I gave him money a number of times, plus gave him drugs to sell to make extra, but come to find out, he was getting high real bad. He kept coming for more and more until I finally put a stop to it. But when I done this, trouble started from him. He started bringing unwanted people to my second house, knowing that was the place I was keeping all the drugs. What got me upset the most was when he brought my wife to the house. This was the turning point when all hell broke lose, tension was everywhere. My wife threatened to call the police and was trying to kill me at the same time. For this, my anger was building in me by the minute for my cousin. Thoughts were running through my head, reminding me of how good I've been to him, but he chosed to turn on me. I became full of turmoil toward him, to the point, I wanted to go knock on his door and kill him right there in the door. The plan was building in my mind more and more to shortened his life. It bothered me so much, I had to tell my father I was getting ready to kill his nephew for what he had done to me. But my father broke it down to me after seeing my anguish, asking me, how will we live together after a terrible thing like that? Then he said I will disown you for life. Even though, I was still furious, Pop gave me something to think about. So I dropped it and went on trying to survive from this dilemma.

The heat was on, things got worst from the pressure of my wife and other drug associates, who had money involved. And in the midst of all this, my mistress and I had started dipping in my own product, we were sniffing and smoking drugs on a regular basics. Not knowing that we were getting addicted, to us it was like drinking a cup of coffee in the mornings. As I had said earlier, things were getting more controversial, so we packed our bags, put our furniture in storage and left toward Atlanta. Again, I asked myself, how can a man get so wrapped up in his own circumstances that he forget his kids? Do this make me less of a man or a man without a purpose? I know one thing, if I would had known God, not just of Him, but known Him personally, I would had chose the right path. I was running around like a piece of paper in a whirlwind, not knowing where I was going.

So we moved to Atlanta with some people she knew that were around their mid fifties. The woman was from New York, who had fled from there because of a busted up drug ring. She was trying to restart her life also, with this country man from Atlanta. He was a hard worker and went to church occasionally. They were real nice in letting us come in with them. My mistress was pregnant now, and we were trying to get adjusted to the place. I was still hustling long distance but things were changing with the little crew I had left. Money were getting mixing and they were getting less dedicated in helping me stay alive. I was losing a lot of money, so finally I had to get a job less than what I was accustom to. Months went by, my mistress was five months pregnant and money were getting real short. All my crew were sprouting out on their own with my money. So I thought about some money I was suppose to pick up, that would have kept me above water. Things were still hectic with my wife at every move so I was making moves so desperately, I exchanged my new 1985 Bronco with the couple's 1968 ninety-eight, in order to go unrecognized. But when my mistress and I had gotten on the outskirts of Greenville, it was a lightly misty rain coming down. I was driving down this country road trying to take a shortcut to my destination, which wasn't very far. I was intending to pick up this check at my credit union and get right back on the highway without going through town. But all of a sudden, halfway on this country road, while driving along with my mistress sitting under my arm, five months pregnant, I kind of edged off the road for a split second. My right tires of this older car hit the edge of the grass. After I seen what was happening, I tried to get back on the road, but it seemed like something was pushing the car like a magnetic force. We went across the road, down this ten feet embankment with the car flipping and chopping down trees until we couldn't move anymore. Right in the middle of nowhere, trees everywhere, there we were trapped in the car. After we came to ourselves we checked each other, then we commenced on trying to get out of the car, fearing it may explode. Both of us checked all the doors and they were jammed, so my mistress panic and tried to kick out the windows but that didn't work either.

Finally, I found a window that came down and as I pulled her out to safety, a paramedic truck was right there on the scene as soon as we got out. They assisted us and put us in the back of the paramedic truck, asking us," how are you all feeling ", and telling us that we were lucky to be alive after chopping down so many trees. I thank God today for saving us when He didn't have to. While we were deep in our sins, the devil was trying to take us out but God turned it around and saved us.

So we ended up at the hospital with my mistress having cracked ribs and the baby was okay and I had stitches in my forehead. On top of all this, I came to find out that my license had been suspended and as soon as I got stitched, the police was waiting to take me to jail. But fortunately, a friend of my mistress came to the rescue by paying my fine and inviting us to stay at her house. We agreed to stay there until my mistress ribs got better. It's sad to say but doing our stay, we would still be indulging in drugs because my mistress friend was getting high too. Her husband didn't know what was going on because he was a nerdy, straight up guy. We really got kind of comfortable there and were overstaying our welcome because we were forgetting that we had to get back to Atlanta to get our belongings. My wife had gotten information to the people we were staying with and about the time we tried to explained to them what had happen, they were already convinced that what we were saying were lies. They were very angry and had no sympathy. So when we went back down to get our stuff, they would not let us have it, even my Bronco. We tried to get the police involved but somehow it didn't work neither. Finally, they moved with everything we owned and we lost it all, so we came back to Greenville, empty handed. After over staying our welcome over her friend house, we moved in with my sister. From a big notorious gangster to a homeless beggar it seemed.

Nevertheless, I still tried to hustle to make money because that was my mindset at the time. Money had gotten scarce, my crew had scattered with my money in their hands. And what upset me the most was, when my right hand man, who supposedly had my back, turned his back on me. Yes, unfortunately he flipped on me too. I guess, I ate my own words when I made the rule with them by not letting a woman come between the business. I was the first to break the rule. My right hand man had taken my money and invested it for himself with my connections. All of the other crew were claiming they lost my money in police raids, including my right hand man. And because I lost everything in Atlanta, including my ride, here I was now asking my right hand man for a favor, more like eating out of his hands, now. From giving him two cars in the past to now, needing one of them to run around in until

I got on feet. But he had the nerves to refuse me, which at the time, I couldn't understand why. But the life we were living was a dirty game and no one was expected to play fair. So I got very angry and pulled out my 44 special right there in broad daylight walking toward him to shoot him. Then some older guys jumped in front of me, telling me it's not worth it. Even his girlfriend tried stopping me because she knew how hurt I was for all the things I had done for him. He was the third person close to me I wanted to shoot, for the same reasons. Thank God that I was stopped! While living this life I was so out of focus, like a wolf running from one end of the forest to the other end, not really accomplishing anything. I had completely forgotten about the family life. I was getting deeper and deeper in my own situation with my mistress right by my side. We had to stay with my sister for a few months and was still getting high on drugs.

Now the drug game was fading away and I was losing all my connections, becoming more of a drug addict than a drug dealer and I didn't even realize it. While living some at my sister and some at the hotels, I met a conman who had a con game going on called "THE PAPER CHASE". Seemingly now, my profession was changing. We got together and came up with one of his schemes to perfect it to it's fullest. He wasn't any rookie at this, he was buying new cars off the lot with no money, he took me to his house he was having built through this paper chasing. He explained to me how we were to operate this caper. I was to go inside the bank dressed like a business man, give the teller a check of the amount of five thousand dollars. Then telling her, I just sold my BMW car to this person and I like to cash this check. At the time, the computers were slow and would only pick up an open account, not showing how much were there. No less than thirty minutes, I was out of there with five thousand in my pocket. I met up with the guy to split the money. This was the first quick money I made without selling drugs. It was a hot deal and my adrenaline was pumping. Then me and my mistress took the money and tried to make more, because that was my thang. So we went to Florida, picked up some drugs to come back to sell. We made more money but my sister called me to tell me the bank called her. They told her they will not lock me up, if I give them the money back. I called them back to set up a time to give their money back. They were very understanding because they made it very clear, they had been looking for the conman who set this up. And said he will surely make time for this caper. It surprised me because I didn't know he was wanted. But by making this move we was back in business. I paid the bank off and started making my runs back to Florida, Atlanta, and New York.

Finally, the baby was born and we invested in an apartment with only a bed for furniture. We stayed there until the baby was a year old, still without furniture. I got myself a job while still hustling on the side, only to keep our habit going, which was getting worst. Our money had gotten really low again, we were living beneath our means. Plus, we were having setbacks from me getting caught driving under suspension. But we kept hanging and striving trying to make it. My mistress was solely depending on me to bring us through. We went to New York and got hooked up by a friend of her family and was back in business again. We even invested in a house and furnished every room but unfortunately, before we could move in good, we were being watched by some narcotic agents. Not knowing that this guy, I was selling to had ratted me out and had brought an agent to our apartment. My mistress was trying to warn me, telling me that something was wrong. But I didn't want to listen because I was looking at the money. When it came to money, I was really blinded. Now I can see very clearly, why that same little boy in the middle of the room, in his little rocking chair was thinking about his future and how he wanted to take over the town of Greenville, was so bad. Anyway we packed the car up to the ream until we were unable to see out the back of the window. And my mistress was steadily telling me, she seen men outside dressed with camouflage suits on, in the woods across the street. But I kept my eyes looking ahead, trying to get to the new home. So after loading the car down, we got on the road but soon as we got mid way through town, we were stopped and surrounded by policemen and narcotic agents. I was sitting on the passenger side holding our baby when they came pointing their guns demanding me to get out slowly. As I was getting out with the baby, they accused me of trying to get her killed. So I asked could I give her to her mother and I slowly did. Now they had me against the car, right in front of the courthouse and probation offices. They told me they had a tip, I had drugs in the car. Then they said, if I tell them where they were, they wouldn't have to tear up the car. Then they threatened me with the news reporters, plus the probationer officers were standing out there looking on too.

My back was against the wall but regardless, I still stood firm and suggested them to do their job, whatever it takes. Then they tried to threatened me again by telling me they will take the baby and put her in DSS service. This time my mistress was disturbed and cried out loud, "tell them where it is". My heart melted after she said that, my bluff was over. They took me to jail and charged me with trafficking and attempt to distribute cocaine with a gun charge and marijuana charge. My mistress was charged with conspiracy and we both had a 100,000 dollar bond. We struggled trying to get out on bond but finally the family members put their properties together and we were freed. This was the worst ordeal we ever went through besides the wreck. We were very worried and stressed out, so my mistress's mother gave us a chapter from the Bible to read, Psalms 121 three times a day to ease our nerves. We done exactly what she said, we would do anything at this point to make things better. We paid our lawyer 5,000 dollars or more and still had problems staying out of jail. But we moved in the house and stayed there a good while. As I was going through the pressures of life, I wasn't noticing my kids in their growing up years. How could you get so wrapped up in your own life and forget about your kids?

THE FAMILY ACROSS TOWN

My wife was applying pressure on us again, so we moved further in the country. We found a house better than where we were. My mistress was working on a good job now and earning good money. Seem like things were turning around again because I had a lot of help from her. But on the other hand, I was drifting off and on my job until finally I lost it. Now things had reversed, she was the sole winner now. But nevertheless, we lived in a different plateau or higher level in our minds, so we thought. We started putting our priorities together and things were picking up, we were handling business correctly.

Then a problem started occurring with me not having a job. I decided to go back to the streets to try to come up within myself, I guess you call it a man thing. I made a little money here and there but the worst thing was that we started slipping again, getting high on the drugs I was bringing home. The problem escalated into a routine situation and it seemed as though, things were getting worst than before. We were calling ourselves slipping around getting high because our daughter who was between three and four at the time and her other daughter who was sixteen was living in the house also. Unaware of them knowing what were going on. We had gotten slack on paying our bills and the rent was getting behind. So we tried to think of other ways to get up money, I even had the audacity to robbed this old drunk man, something totally against my nature. But it got to the point of desperation and stupidity. I first seen the old drunk man in the checkout line in the grocery store with his wallet wide open with nothing but hundreds. So I told my mistress to go get the truck that we borrowed from a friend guy of hers because I had my vehicle repossessed. Anyway, as the old guy moved toward the door and preceded outdoors, I quickly followed him out and approached him for a light for my cigarette. As soon as he went in his pocket, I grabbed his wallet and threw him on the ground. I ran toward the truck and jumped in the bed of the truck laying down until we got home. As soon as we got to the house, the police was riding through the neighborhood flashing their lights through windows of people houses. So we cut off the lights and laid in the floor until they were long gone. This was one of the worst things I've ever done, this state of mine I was in, wasn't me. I sometimes wondered how could a man change and become so desperate that he'll do anything.

When I used to go to make the trips to Florida, the older women that were at the spot, would tell me I had too good of a nature to be in the drug game. The same came from guys in jail, who knew me growing up, told me that they thought I was going to be a doctor or lawyer, the way I was raised but what happened. After that scene, we pushed on like nothing had happen with things getting worst as the days went by. I was going over people houses getting high, while baby-sitting my little girl. Several times or more, my mistress would leave her job to come to hunt me down and would find me too. We were getting in so bad of a condition that we were using and abusing family members and close friends. When we came around, people would freeze up like we had a disease and we became a regular Bonnie and Clyde to society, our reputation were spreading widely. And the sad thing about the whole ordeal, our daughter was getting the worst end out of all this mess. Another bad thing I would do, was convince myself I could make a comeback with just one more package. The devil continued convincing me of this comeback and keeping me blinded from seeing the truth, that I was addicted and needed help.

One of the worst scenarios occurred when my mistress's mother wanted some land down by where we were staying. She was staying in New York and wanted to move South. She entrusted her daughter with five thousand dollars to put on the land. It was surely at the wrong time when this money came in this household. Ideas rumbled through my head a hundred miles a minute. I couldn't rest knowing that the money was in the house. Satan was feeding my mine with thoughts of a serious comeback and we were so behind on bills. At first, I tried to talk her into letting me invest some of the money but she refused. So one day when she was sleep under some medication, I took it on my own to take twenty-five hundred dollars to invest on drugs. I thought I was back in business but only to be fooled by my own greediness. I lost money in the streets and got high on the side. My mistress was highly upset and had to join me to keep from going overboard. She was repeatedly taken medication and I repeatedly gave in to my own greediness. So now, I went after the other twenty-five hundred dollars and again it didn't work out. Now she was really mad, to the point of having a nervous breakdown. She stabbed me and threatened to kill me but to save her the trouble, I took a large bottle of Advil pills trying to commit suicide. Even that didn't work, I believe sometimes God will let you live to make you deal with your problems.

We went on confused and in despair from losing the money and plus going through the agony of her mother. Everyway we were turning, we were losing. We lost our house our furniture again and had to live with my sister again. Until we finally found another house and lived there without furniture and lost it and ended up in an apartment and lived there without furniture and lost it too. During all this, we had our daughter who was growing older and my mistress other daughter also. But before we left this last apartment I had started the conman business again. I went through town using fake identifications to steal money from loan companies and anywhere else I could get money. My mistress was going in department stores stealing and I would go back in the same store and sell it right back to them, sort of speak. We done our devious capers until I was being investigated by some detectives, who finally caught up with me and arrested me. I stayed in jail for forty-five days without bond until they took me to court. And while I was in there, I found Jesus and the Holy Spirit this time. The judge charged me with five counts of pertaining money under false pretense with a ten year suspended sentence on each count and five years probation. The judge also warned me, if I get a similar charge again, I'll get fifty years. But when I came home I was full of the Holy Ghost, I was really feeling different. After seeing this empty apartment and seeing my mistress still on her quest bringing in drugs, seemingly worst. I tried to stop it but I guess, not hard enough. I was finally back indulging again, putting the Bible down and getting back on the rampage. What keeps a person continuously falling back in the same mess, not being aware of the failure of it or not caring? Or why does a person keep living in despair, not having a clue about the future, it doesn't even phase you. I believe a person is blinded by his own desires and satan takes over to keep you trapped in a world of lust and everything in it.

Now I have really seen the Scriptures fulfilled in Matthew 13:19-22, when I first got Saved, I heard the Word of the Kingdom and didn't understand it. Then the wicked one came and snatched away what was sown in my heart. This is he who received seed by the wayside. Then there's another, when I was going in and out of jail, getting what they call jailhouse religion. I was getting the religion and trying to preach to others when I wasn't rooted myself. This was because I received the seed on stony ground. This is he who hears the Word and immediately received it with joy. Yet has no root in himself and endures only for a little while. For when tribulation or persecution arises because of the Word, immediately he stumbles. Here's another, when I had received the Holy Spirit and came back in the same mess, I quickly went back to that mess, because now I received the seed among thorns and heard the

Word but the cares of this world and the deceitfulness of riches and drugs choked the Word, so I was unfruitful.

My mistress had ran into some money from an accident settlement, which abled us to get another apartment with furniture. She also bought a Mercedes about seven or eight years old. We were doing alright, our daughter was in the fourth or fifth grade. Slowly we started drifting back on drugs again, it was getting so bad that we were lending our car to get drugs. We were even stealing from the stores again, selling the merchandise back to the same stores. We were making sometimes three hundred to five hundred dollars a trip, just to put it back into drugs. Before we lost this apartment my father died with Asthma, the same day we were getting high. My brother-in-law came to our door to let us know my father had just died. I didn't know what to do because we were in the middle of trying to figure out how to get some more drugs. But the more I came to myself, I began to fall apart so I rushed to the hospital where all my family were. As I looked at my father laying there, I felt so wrong knowing that I had been getting high all morning, I felt like I was responsible since I was the only boy in the family. My mind was so twisted now but after the funeral my mistress and I continued on, trying to make it the best way we could with our problem. Finally, we lost our apartment and had to move in with her daughter, who was old enough to have her own apartment. It was in a drug infested area so this didn't make it any better neither, we got even worst until we had to split.

IS IT EVER GONNA STOP

My father had just died and my mother was having a hard time adjusting in the house alone. So I decided to move in with her, since I didn't have anywhere else to go. I thought to myself, now that my mistress and I have departed from each other, things should get better for the both of us. Because we were good with each other in supporting our crime activities but we weren't good for each other as for focusing on our problems. I had got a job and was going to church with my mother, trying to do the right thing. But it was still to soon for me to have all the wildness out of me because I was sneaking out on payday dipping and dabbing doing my thing. I was making it a habit every week until my mother started seeing it with her own eyes. We would have heated confrontations of my problems to the point of me being put out. But one thing for sure, I would never steal from my mother. I would steal from myself but never my mother unless I spent up my payroll check before giving her anything, thank God I never reached that point with her. The reason I said this was because when you are fully wrapped up in them drugs you are not responsible in your mind. That "crack" is from the pits of hell and it delivers your mind in the pits of hell, also.

During our departure from each other, our daughter mostly stayed with her at first until my mistress started leaving her over other people houses, for days. My daughter would call me and asked have I seen her mother, so I would go get her and keep her with me. And my mistress would always come back to get her, after she had come off her benges. We had gotten back together several times, hoping we could make it work for our daughter's sake. But time after time, it resolved to the same situations. It was a funny thing how we got back together this last time. Here I was trying to get back on feet my own way, working and hustling and doing pretty good with myself. When one day I was riding through town and who do I see walking down the street but my mistress. I turned around to give her a ride and asked her where was she going, she said she didn't have a definite destination so we started hanging out again. One thing led to another until we were back trying it again. This time, we were going to different people houses, staying awhile getting high and selling drugs and moving on. I had quit my job by hanging back in the streets again. Things were getting pretty bad again, my mother had our daughter so we knew she was being taken care of. We were running out of places to lay our head so we finally got us an apartment from some money we ran up on. Only furniture we had, was a twin sleeper sofa and a mattress for our daughter who was in middle school now and was back with us. But just like all the other times, things just didn't work out, it got worst instead of better. We ended it this time with a terrible fight. This was it, I went back home to mom and she went her way but ended up in jail for a year. I took our daughter in with me and my mother and I kept her the rest of the way.

I was close to forty now and my daughter was in high school and it was very much over due for me to be settling down. But I still had this mentality in me of being a gangster or as the young boys call it being thuggish. This is one of the worst roads a person can go on because there's not a career or future in it. And believe me, if you haven't found out yet you will. Brothers and sisters, I learned later on in life that our deepest fear is not that we are inadequate. Our deepest fear is that we are powerful beyond measure. We ask ourselves who am I to be brilliant, gorgeous, talented and fabulous, actually who are you not to be. We were born to make manifest the Glory of God that is within us. And as we let our light shine we unconsciously give others the permission to do the same. As I was saying before, the thuggish life is no future and usually ends in destruction.

One of my last encounters on the streets, almost had been my last, for real. I had a few attempts on my life but this one was too close. Some teenagers that appeared to be clean-cut guys, tried to rob me. I was out one night, trying to make a comeback on some money I had lost, getting high. I started from $35 dollars and had gotten up to $200 dollars, close to what I'd lost. The hour was about 2:00 o' clock in the morning, when I made my third trip back to this spot, I was getting help from, but the guys I were dealing with had left. So I asked these teenagers for help, who had took over the late shift, probably for guys like me. They tried to lure me in a dark alley but I wouldn't go. Then the one I was talking to, pulled out an automatic pistol to my forehead and pulled the trigger but it jammed. I turned and commenced to run, then he hit me in the back of my head. I was unconscious for a minute or two, and as I was coming back conscious again, I felt them going in my pockets and beating on me at the same time. So I managed to get on my feet and swinging at the same time until I was able to run. It was about six of them and they ran me until they realized they couldn't catch me. I was a bloody mess and I still have the scars to this day. I guess this had to happen because of the time I rob this old drunk man. Like people say what goes around comes around. I believe this was God's way of justifying what I had done. I'm just glad the gun didn't go off between my eyes and I thank God today, for His mercy and grace.

That night after getting away, I didn't know where to go except to this drug infested hotel where I mostly hung out, trying to sell my drugs. Some girls I knew, help me stop bleeding and we hung out all night partying off the money, they didn't get. When I came home the next day, I was still bruised up and my shirt was filled with blood. My daughter came to the door and broke out crying. I felt so bad for breaking her heart, I promised her right there, I was giving the streets up. At this time, I came out the streets and started going back to church. I found a job and was enjoying family gatherings again. My life was coming back together, I still had that wildness from the streets in me but I was staying away from them and learning how to live civilized again. This job I was on, was a place I'd worked before so I knew a lot of people there. I really enjoyed this job, talking to everyone who would listen and flirting with the women, like I had it going on. But only perpetrating because this was a time I was getting myself back together.

Then I ran into this woman at work, who was unique within herself. She was a homely christian girl, a woman of morals and standards. When I set my eyes to her eyes a different sting went through me. I would always be on break when she was. I even tried to convince myself that she was not my style, and she already had told me, she could never date me or give me a half of a chance and the reason why she said this was because a few of her friends were joking about me and her getting together. But somehow or another we became closer and closer. The force got stronger and stronger until we finally connected and started dating. She was an extraordinary woman and kept me in balance because I was from one extreme to the next. She was also serious about her walk with God and had been celibate for four years. At this time, I didn't know what celibacy really was and to be honest, I didn't know what being born again was neither. I knew I had been Saved some twenty years ago but I didn't understand it. With the savvy and wildness I still had in me, I went after her like I didn't have nothing to lose and we finally came together in intimacy. She was teaching me and giving me wise counsel of the Word.

She was sharing her love unconditionally, in which I was trying to return my love to her. It was kind of hard because I had made up my mind before, to never give my love up again and get serious with anyone. From dealing with the different women, including my wife and mistress, I was blaming all of them for my problems. Not knowing at the time, I made the problems for myself. But by dealing with this young lady, I was gradually moving into the christian world, so I thought. I even went by this christian store and bought christian T-shirts and a collection of T.D Jakes DVDs, concerning Maximizing the Moment. And from listening to the DVD with T.D. Jakes preaching about Elijah and Elisha, I was determine that I wasn't going back to the streets because I was burning my Ox. One day after coming from church, in which were filled with the Holy Spirit, I took my girlfriend and sisters to a nice restaurant. I was feeling so good that I told them I was never, going back in the streets again. With me not knowing the Holy Spirit and understanding how He works, that was an understatement I shouldn't have made. But I was feeling so confident of my state of mind at the time. My living standards were getting better, I even had established a checking account which was totally off limits for me.

But not long after I made that statement, for some reason or another I needed some money and I heard about this check cashing place. So, I went to cash a personal check there. It was so easy I went to another then another then another until I was chasing money again. Then desperate ideas went through my head once again, I was out to the races. The first thing came to my mind was, if I could, just cash enough checks to get some drugs to sell, I could get out of this hole, I had dug. And I done just that, except things got worst instead of better. Here I was again, back selling drugs on the side, and trying to keep it confidential away from my mother and girlfriend. Everyday, I would get off work and spend some time on the block. The more I hung out, the more I wanted to hang out. One of my partners, who started off with me in the beginning and who I almost shot in the mix, had came back on my side, even though he was on the dyanalysis machine suffering from a bad kidney. We joined up for the same reasons and that was to renew our vows in finishing what we started before. Satan will really have you living a false dream if you allow him. He knows our weaknesses and uses it to trick us to going around in that terrible circle again and again.

Anyway, my partner and I met on the block everyday. It was like old times, with me running things. We were determine to make a comeback. We charged the block like a hurricane or a rushing water, whereabouts, a dam had broke. Everybody knew what we were doing on the block, we weren't hiding anything. Two old cats, thirty-nine and forty years old, trying to out do the young thugs on their level. I guess, that's why the old saying says, "ain't nothing worst than an old fool". We done our thang and were good at it, but the only problem we had were that we done better than anybody on the block, then at the end of the day, we'll find a spot to get high. We didn't intend to do much but everytime we would talk ourselves in, and couldn't get out. I was the worst one, my partner would beg me to stop and say, "let's go". And I would put him off a little longer until we didn't have anything for the next day. Then we'll start from scratch and come back up just to go back down. It was an ongoing cycle. We were the most talked about folks on the block. So many things went on, on the block, I can just write a book on the block.

My girlfriend had got suspicious and my mother had an idea, but I thank God for a praying mother. I had came completely out the church and I was missing important dates with my girlfriend. Just like, on her birthday I was a day or two late, dirty and smelling because I hadn't changed clothes for two or three days. I just didn't have sense to stop or come back out of the streets. The devil really had me blind, I couldn't see no further than where I was. It was liked being in quicksand, the more I moved the more I sunk.

Then one day, when I was out on the block, my mother called me to tell me, a detective had came by looking for me. He left me a number to get in touch with him so I done just that. When I spoke with him on the phone, he asked me to come down to his office to talk with him. At first I said to myself or you crazy, but he told me I didn't have any alternative and it was for my best interest. So I went down to his office and he went over the charge with me and then, he let me go, giving me the impression that it was nothing. I went back to doing what I was doing. A year went by and they finally brought it back to surface. The courts sent me a card to come to court. Then, I checked with the solicitor and she told me it was to my advantage to get a lawyer. Time was beginning to run out and the solicitor was threatening to give me ten to twenty years. So I got my old good lawyer friend, who use to get me out of trouble before. He knew just about everybody in the judicial system. But when he took my case, he told me, the solicitor was seeking the maximum and he didn't know her but he heard she was rough and didn't play no games. Now I was getting disturbed, so I told my lawyer I wanted a jury trial because I didn't believed they had me on tape. We went back and forth for two months. I even tried to put them off for another year but they weren't hearing it. My mother was getting upset too, she stuck with me though, no matter what I took her through, she was always there.

Finally, it was court time and anticipation was growing more and I was bargaining as much as I could. My girlfriend showed me much love in this ordeal, she also stuck with me regardless of the situation. My girlfriend and I marched around that lobby all day trying to get answers to relieve the problem. I was still trying to prolong it by saying I wanted a jury trial. But my lawyer sit me down and told me, I wouldn't want a jury trial because if they found me guilty I could get up to thirty years. Then he told me, the solicitor was already pushing for at least ten years but he knew the judge. So he suggested that if I take the guilty plea it might not be so bad. He also told me to stop giving him money because they are not delaying anymore and they are going to give me a sentence. He told me that because I was still asking for probation or house arrest. I didn't want to make any time in prison but I had to accepted it. But my name was too far down the list, so I didn't get called that day. We all went home quietly and separated quietly.

I suddenly started preparing myself for the worst. I had won fifteen hundred dollars from a baseball bet, so I distributed some to my mother and my girlfriend. Then I took my old hoopty car which I had and sold it to a young thug, I use to deal with pretty much. I drove up in his backyard, while him and another guy was sitting in his car smoking a blunt. I told him about my situation and he bought the car right on the spot. He drove me home and we listened to Tupac while smoking a blunt. I asked them, to let me stop at the store to get a double deuce Icehouse beer. Knowing in my heart, I was going to prison the next day. I really didn't know this was the last time, I would be with the boys. I gave my last farewell to them when I got out of the car. I came in the house blunted up and still feeling empty and worried. I went straight in and put Tupac new CD on. By listening to Tupac CD, unveiling drama and being high from the blunt, and while drinking a beer, it really relaxed my mind and made me feel up to facing reality. It was no comparison to going to church earlier that week with a complexed mind, feeling nobody understood what I was going through. I first went to the church where my family attended but with my mind being heavily burdened, it caused me not to enjoy the service. Then I left there right in the middle of service and went over to my girlfriend church. It was the same way, I couldn't get into it neither. As I was saying earlier, you can't compare the two. During the time when I was going to church regularly, I didn't have church in me. I was far from the Holy Spirit, not knowing Him at all. That's why, I found relaxation in Tupac, a blunt and a beer because that's what I had in me. I had more street wisdom in me than God's Wisdom, that's why I couldn't understand the church. It wasn't that the church couldn't understand me, it was me confused.

Early the next morning about eight o'clock AM I arose, not knowing I was beginning to enter into a "miraculous" destiny of a new beginning. I got up, embraced myself and took a deep breath. I begun to prepare myself mentally and physically. My mother and I got in the car and drove with complete silence until she made the statement, maybe they'll put you on probation. I told her in an assuring voice, no mama, I think I'm going in this time. Finally, we arrived at the courtroom and we went to the second floor and there standing in the lobby was my lawyer asking me, have I made up my mind yet, rather I wanted a jury trial or the guilty plea. I looked him in the eye and told him I wanted the guilty plea. He made a sigh of relief and said good, I know this judge in spite of the solicitor trying to give you ten years or more, I might can get you lesser. So I nodded my head and said lets do it.

We walked in the courtroom, took our seat and waited patiently for our turn. When the judge called my name, my heart fell to my knees. After hearing the judge reciting my charge, he directed his next question toward me, asking me what do I think about the charge. I told him with all sincerity, I would like probation or house arrest so I can stay at home with my daughter. Then after I spoke, he looked at my lawyer to hear what he had to say. My lawyer knowing they were going to lock me up, asked for the least time possible, using my daughter in conversation to have consideration. The judge quickly said without a shout of a doubt, three years. My mother burst out with a loud cry and while they were putting the handcuffs on me, I was trying to calm her down by reassuring her I was going to be alright but she cried even more. After seeing her break down the way she did, it reminded me of all the times I had let her down, going in and out of jail and back and forth in the courtrooms. I was trying not to feel any weakness but it was like holding a flood in, that needed to come out. Nevertheless, I held my grounds because of where I was. But I still couldn't help for thinking how a mother's love is, unconditional like God's love. No matter what I've took her through, she still showed much love.

DELIVERANCE

This miraculous transformation of a journey begins while waiting in a small holding cell until court was over. Soon as court was over, the officer came and took us through the normal procedure to prepare us to get on the prison van by putting us in shackles. I was talking in a rebellious spirit to the officers and complaining and joking every step of the way. Finally, arriving to the Detention center to get booked in, I was still giving out smart comments and complaining trying to cover up the emptiness, I was really feeling. I got put up for the night and early the next morning at four o'clock AM, I was called to move out, otherwords, get your stuff and lets ride. So a group of us were called to line up on the wall to get shackled and like before I was still giving out smart remarks.

This time we got on a huge bus and road about twenty-five minutes to a maximum security facility. One that I had been to before, just to come for a few weeks or for a month in lock-up, to get physicals and go through orientation. But this time it was different we just stayed there for one day. They had moved R&E to another facility about one hundred miles away. So we finally arrived at this facility and got checked in. This place was something new to me because I guess, I haven't been this far out of town in the system before. But things were coming back to me again, I thought I wouldn't see a place like this again but unfortunately, here I go again. They put me in a cell a little smaller than a bedroom with double beds, one on top of the other, more like bunkbeds, with a toilet and sink. The only thing that was wrong, the jail system was full and the room called for two people and I was the third. That meant I had to sleep on the floor across from the toilet. It even came for a moment, when it was four in the same room, two on the floor and two in the bed. It was like a rotation, whenever one move on, in the system, the next one in line gets the better choice of bedding. Fortunately, everybody got alone with each other real well, whites and blacks.

It was pretty crowded though, with a toilet and a small window. When someone had to use the bathroom, we would roll over and cover our heads and tell the person to flush a lot. We were able to take a shower every other day. Now this was lock-up, where you stay until they get you into the system, where they want you to go. I mind you, they had one shower on each floor with about thirty to forty guys to one shower. They let us out the cell about an hour or two to take turns. We made our own recreation right there on the concrete on the inside, half of the day. The biggest drive that drove us were tobacco. We weren't allowed to smoke and that made it worst because we craved it even more. We figured, being a criminal already, it wasn't hard breaking the law for some tobacco, so we had an underground system going on. In this block, which was called B-block, everybody came to know one another. Everybody from different walks of life, so everybody tried to make it as pleasant as possible. We went outside to go to breakfast, lunch and dinner and sometimes they let us stretch our legs and sit in the grass to soak up some sunshine.

One of my best friends was lock up on a drug charge also, three weeks prior to my arrest. So I asked a few guys that might have knew him and they said he had left two weeks before I got there. I was pretty sure, I was going to run into him there just to have somebody close to hang with but I was wrong. Everyday it was a hustle and bustle to where and who had the "smokes", actually tobacco in a bag. I was in the cell with two white guys, one of them was a red head freckle face guy who looked like he wouldn't harm a fly. But he was in for accessory to arm robbery and was slapped with a ten year sentence. The other guy who looked like the Clark Kent type was in for his second go around for pallunia capers, mainly for smoking crack. And he came from a rich family by the way he was talking. We all would tell our stories and experiences we had, then it would get quiet.

After awhile, literature was being passed out concerning Jesus Christ. And we already had a guy on the block preaching out loud at times and introducing himself as Rev. And also, doing the quiet time of the evening after dinner, everybody would calm down in our cells, some would be reading and some playing cards. But mostly it was reading, at least in our cell. I believe everybody's mind goes into deep concentration of reformation sometimes of another. Most of the reading material was about the Word of God and maybe a few novels. But I begun to read everyday, books about the Word and to be honest, it was kind of kicking in too. The freckle face guy finally moved on and another guy came in his place. I was able to move in a bed spot now. This guy was full of fire and wild stories, he was a little bit older than me. He was a black guy with freckles also and was always talking about how much money he was making on computer scams. Nevertheless, in the calm of the day, he was joining us in reading also.

The Rev had started giving Bible studies each day. I would ease out there slowly just to hear what he was speaking about. From all the reading I was doing, I ran up on a scripture of John the Baptist and I felt a strong feeling, this man called Rev was similar to John the Baptist. The more I heard him, the more I wanted to hear him, he was bold and tenacious with the Gospel. He spoke out loudly, quoting the scriptures, even if you didn't want to hear it. It was as though, he was planted there for such a time. We kindled a little closer, everytime lunch or dinner came, instead of sitting with strangers, I would look for him or be with him. Every word was full of fire, sometimes I tried to calm him down but he would get worst. The little Bible studies he was giving were growing bigger. Everybody would come out of their cells one by one and sit on the concrete to commence to listen to what he had to say. He had everybody's full attention because the bigger the crowd the more he preached. But even at times, he would have conflicts with some of the guys, sometimes it would get so bad he would get into deep arguments. People would try to judge him wrongly but somehow I always looked at the situation differently. At the time, I didn't know how satan comes in the midst of a situation to try to turn people against you but this was what was happening. Finally, the system was moving people again and Rev got shipped to another place. And everybody were back to normal chasing tobacco and playing cards.

I was getting impatient because it was going on thirty days, when most people was moving in twenty days. I was getting agitated to the point where I was questioning the officers and demanding for answers, why so long? Then finally my day came, I was in the line up. They told me to pack my bags and I done just that and when they say pack your bags, that's exactly what they mean because they give you a brown paper grocery bag with all your stuff in it. I got my mat and sheets and got behind some more guys that were leaving. We all gathered in a big cafeteria room and were sanction out like cattle. Everybody in separate groups going to different places, shackled from waist to feet. But it didn't matter because I was happy for leaving there to go to a place where I heard my best friend was. As the buses came, they were marching us to it, to get on board, then all of a sudden the lady officer called me back. I went to see what she wanted and to tell her to hurry up before I miss my ride. Little that I knew, she was canceling my trip anyway. She told me, "you couldn't go there so get those chains taken off of you and get your stuff and report back to your cell". I was confused and upset, asking her why the change but she said, all she knew was that I was getting kicked back out of the system, everytime she tried to put it back in. Being highly disappointed, I turned going back to my cell sadly. One of the guys I knew from the streets told me, while I was walking through the yard, he had seen this happen before and told me to get comfortable because you are going to be here awhile. He said it usually take up to two weeks or a month to get me back on the moving books again. Then I was really upset but I couldn't do anything about it.

I came back to the block I was in and everybody asked me what happen? So I told them and laid my stuff down without unpacking and went to a corner of the block that was facing outside, I looked toward the sky asking the Lord, why me? Why do everything goes wrong with me? Then I asked Him to help me please and show me why I'm always suffering. So I turned from there to go back to my room and I spreaded my bed out, in which the guys had thought I had left so they had my bunk. I spreaded my bed on the floor, when one of the guys came running to tell me, they were calling my name up front to go all the way. I told him, man that can't be because they just sent me back here. He was determine, that's what it was but I told him I was going to lay it down. Then an officer came and asked me my name, then he asked me, did I want to go? I said yes, then he said, "so get your stuff and go". I went back in front of the same lady officer and asked her what happen this time, she repeatedly said, she didn't know just go. At this point, little that I knew, this was the turning point of my life. As I was riding on the bus to my destination, I couldn't help for thinking how things went down and how God came for my rescue in that quick instance. It was a long ride and every step of the way, my heart was overflowed with joy. Just contemplating on how good God is and how He's able to change things, it made my ride much easier. Plus, I was going on a yard where my best friend was.

Finally, we arrived after two hours of riding, they took off our shackles and put us in a holding tank. For a whole week or two we went through what they called orientation, learning about their system and getting more check-ups and getting our bedding equipment. After I got situated I walked around trying to see who I knew and by surprise, I hardly knew anyone. The next day I was going to dinner and passed right by my best friend without recognizing him. He spoke to me saying, "oh you don't know nobody now huh". I looked around and I declare he was two shades darker with a weight lost of about forty pounds. I asked, what is wrong with you, are you alright, man you look different. We shook hands and hugged and I felt a whole lot better because there was someone there I could relate with now. Then out of the clear blue here comes the Rev walking up with a big smile on his face. We done the same thing shook hands and hugged one another. I told him,

I didn't know you came down here too. I asked him, are you still teaching and preaching and giving Bible studies? He answered yes, then he said, I don't be playing. Soon as Rev welcomed me in, he quickly got to business and took me under his wing. I mean everyday from morning to evening we would walk or sit around the yard going over the Bible. It was though, he was assigned to teach me.

My best friend had started going to church on a regular basis. He also met Rev on several occasions and his complaint was that Rev was too persistent, that he talked about the Lord too much. I would try to split my time between the two but I always leaned back toward Rev. He had a burning sensation in him that I was yearning for and had to have it. Each day on the yard was different, even though there was no where to go, it was always a different situation going on. Some days were harder, where the adversary would have everyone in rage, other days, everything would be peaceful and smooth, everybody got alone in their own activities. Now the days were pushing on and Rev was checking on me more regularly. He would come early in the morning before I got up, wherefore, we'll walk around the track talking about the Word, while he'll be quoting scripture. He said exercise was good for the soul. Then during lunch we'll come together again, going to a picnic table to have Bible study. We would get out our little Testament and really get down. He always made the subject so meaniful, wherefore I had to come back out during dinner time to finish up. Seem like the more I got with him the more I began to read and search for myself.

I had a couple of room dawgs who were totally opposite, they were wondering themselves, what was going on. I was going to the Chapel spending time on my own, listening to tapes of preachers, mostly T.D. Jakes. I had gotten to a point where I would try to listen to every tape they had on T.D. Jakes. I was getting where, I was desiring the presence of the Lord by being in the Chapel because it was so peaceful. The Bible study on the yard was getting larger, guys were coming with outstanding knowledge of the Lord. Their knowledge were so outstanding that it caused confusion. Everybody wanted to be the greatest between the guys that had been there the longest. Animosity was taking over the yard between the elders of the saints, even Rev was going through strife with them. It was so much controversy, I was disappointed with them all, even Rev. So I started seeking my own peace and revelation. I went to the Chapel every chance I had to read or listen to T.D.Jakes. I felt so peaceful there until the elders brought that mess inside of the Chapel. They were violently speaking against each other to the point, I had to speak out about where they were, for God sakes.

What was the most glorious and beautifullest thing that happen, came from an innocent, quiet little black lady who was one of the Chaplains. I've never heard her say, five words together but I finally got to hear her preach, I didn't know she could preach. She blew the top of the building off. The Holy Spirit was upon her so strong, she was like a total different person from her personality and it was all good. She preached out of Genesis 11 and Acts 2 and it was a powerful message. She stunned everyone, her title was, "This mess just don't make no sense". She started out saying, everybody is running around the Chapel thinking he's smarter than the next guy and talking about one another. You better get your souls right because if God can change tongues in one group of smart men in Genesis 11, to turn their whole agenda around and then come back in the New Testament and bring a group of men tongues together, where at first they had separate languages but now they had the same. Then she said to the congregation, what do you think He can do to you all, who think its all about you. After this sermon, it wasn't the same anymore, I believe she stirred up something in the heavenly realm. She certainly gave everybody in that service something to think about. I was so glad, joy ran out my skin.

One day after not seeing each other for a while, Rev convinced me that we had to get together. So we were hanging out again, studying even deeper. He was really working with me, making me see the light. In between times my best friend and I hung out playing basketball and jogging. We also would sit in the grass and talk about some deep subjects. He had convinced himself, he was not selling drugs anymore and he was going to continue going to church, plus get married as soon as he get out. He would often tell me, he couldn't see why I hung out with Rev so much. Then he told me, Rev was to religious and to bold with it and Rev just can't be going up to folks talking about the Lord. Then he said, some people don't want to here that stuff. I told him, I believe we were good for each other with my mildness and his boldness, plus I was learning a lot from him.

The days went on and other inmates were telling me and my best friend Mike, we had six months or better before they consider on moving anybody. The inmates said, once you get on this yard they forget about you. Mike wanted so badly to go back toward home and would not accept what they were saying. Mike told me, he was staying away from negative thinking people. Now Mike had been on this yard three weeks to a month prior to me coming here. I had been on the yard for a month now so it was Mike's second month. He told me he was having faith in God to remove him off this yard and he didn't care what the other inmates were saying. Now I have to remind you or have I mentioned that this was the same guy who hustled drugs with me right before we caught this bid and I haven't never heard him say anything about God. But he stuck with his faith and he was moved to another camp in less than a weeks' time. It was so amazing, I became overwhelmed with the reaction from his faith. I waved with gladness for him and loniness for me as he walked out the door to his new destiny. The place was a little closer, not like he'd wished, but it was better than where he was. I wondered for days, how faith moved Mike, so I girded up my loins and started proclaiming the same faith. I was telling Rev I was going closer to home too, in Jesus name. Rev would make sure I said in the name of Jesus.

Believe me in a weeks time, Rev and I was standing around the basketball court watching a game. And all of a sudden, my name came across the loud speaker telling me to report to the front. I told Rev, what in the world do they want now. He told me, they might be calling you to go closer to home. But to keep myself from getting disappointed, I told Rev, it's probably a case worker or something. I paraded up front and gave them my name, then they told me I had been transferred to another camp. When they gave me the paper, I asked them, whereabouts am I going, they told me, a place called Livesay, which was a camp thirty minutes from home. I was so happy, I could've jumped to the ceiling and I thanked the Lord that much more, remembering the faith Mike had and what Rev told me, with faith of a mustard seed God will move mountains. Rev and I celebrated together with laughter and praises to the Lord. But soon after the celebration, we looked at each other in a farewell stare. I admitted to him, how much I was going to miss him, so I started trying to get information to keep communication with each other, when we both get on the outside. I gave him my phone number and address at home and he only gave me his inmate number. He told me he didn't have an address or phone number to give me. But he said, write me here and maybe when I get out, I'll come where you are.

The day had drawn near for me to leave and Rev continued to give me Gospel counsel. He told me that I was going closer to home and that could mean more problems because I was going around some of my familiar, rowdy friends. He told me, not to let all I have learned slip away from me, when I get there find some more Christians folks to hang around with. Then he took me to a scripture that said, "there's One who is closer than a brother". He reminded me, if you don't have no one to turn to, you can turn to Jesus because He'll stick with you when nobody else will. This was surely a teary moment for both of us. God had really soften my heart and I believe everybody has a little tenderness in their heart, no matter how hard a person try to be.

I tell you, I'm glad I allowed God to soften my heart. Sometimes God will soften your heart against your own will and that's good too, because some of us are so stubborn and hard hearted. The most thing I could give Rev was my canteen, which was food. And he was most gladly for it because I was already sharing all my canteen with him anyway, simply because of him not having any contact on the outside. Now I had already contacted my family and told them the good news which was a relief for my mother and my girlfriend from traveling so far. Rev stood waving, saying goodbye and still giving me Godly counsel. I told him I will surely write but I tried to write him and never got a response. Unto this day, I truly believed that he was an Angel assigned to me.

The Livasay Experience Part Two Of Deliverance:

Traveling back close to home on this three hour journey, I couldn't hold myself from rejoicing, thinking of the greatness of being back close to home. Arriving at the place, I immediately grasped the fresh air with a deep breath, which seemed much differently than where I was. As I was getting checked in at the front desk, my anxiety was coming on more and more to get on the yard and see who I knew. Finally, as we were walking to our assigned room, I was constantly looking around with excitement trying to see who I knew and to my surprise I didn't see anyone I knew. So I went and put up my gear and quickly went to the yard to look around to scope everybody out. Finally, I ran into some guys I knew who was really broke in and settled and knew all the ropes. Through these few guys I was learning the way, the system ran things there. They had a lot of street wisdom in them and they were some of the fastest ones on the yard. But as I was hanging around some of them, my mind was going back to the Wateree experience with Rev, my tutor and friend. I couldn't help for thinking of what he told me when I was leaving and for some reason I couldn't get it off of my mind. He told me not to forget to find some Bible studying, church going, christian fellows who love the Lord, to hang around with, when I get to where I was going. I remembered him telling me temptation will be waiting at the door because I'll be closer to home and back around my street buddies. So immediately I got back to reading everynight and when day came I searched for some christian fellows.

I attended church and seen guys gathered in their own little groups but I wasn't connecting. One day, I was singing a gospel song in the restroom and a guy from the choir heard me and invited me to a practice. I turned him down, then I told him I can't sing, plus, I've never been on a choir before. But he insisted that I come even if just to sit in for a night. So I sit in with them one night and got acquainted with some of the guys. Two days later, the guy who asked me to sit in with them went home and this was when I found out that he was the lead singer for the group. I kind of eased around, trying to get to know the guys and they finally convinced me to join. I thought, why not because since the lead singer left, these guys wasn't any better than me. Each time we came together it became more fellowshipping than practice, we would exclude the practice at times and have Bible study. I was enjoying the moment more and more, I was mostly thrilled being apart of something pure and clean. So I was now hanging around some of the leaders of the gospel group. They were deeper into the Word than the rest of us, two of them, especially. The three of us worked in the kitchen together, they were chefs and I cleaned tables. We became closer, we song and we fellowshipped all the day long. One of the guys was named Walt and the other was named Dee. They were top-notched in the Word and kept me lined up with the Word. I was feeling real comfortable hanging around christian fellows for a change. Even though, I had been going through a personal thing with God concerning Him speaking to me about different changes of my life and actually having a teacher previously teaching me how to study and staying focus, I still didn't consider myself of being a christian. And the kitchen seemed like the worst place to keep your salvation, everyday in the kitchen was a struggle with all the different personalities. Even Walt and Dee were having a lot of difficulties in there, they were rebuking demons all over the place. It had gotten to the point where demons were being more recognized than Jesus.

I continued studying at night and going to church functions during the day, in spite of being put in the most notorious dorms on the yard. These fellows in this dorm were on work release and they were accessed to going on the streets so they had a lot of tricks going on. A few of us were put in there when we first step foot on the yard because of limited space. You usually have to work yourself up to this point in time but I thought this was the place to be simply because they had better living quarters, plus, this was the dorm closer to getting out. But from living in this notorious dorm and working in the kitchen with all types of attitudes, personalities and confusion, I still had the Lord on my mind and in my situation. Seemed like it was something down inside of me that reminded me of everything I was doing. No matter how much I studied, I still had that other half in me that kept a relationship with the slicksters. Sometimes I would get tire of studying and go into the TV room where everybody hung out, just to smoke a cigarette or two and to hang long enough to shoot a little breeze with them. Then God was beginning to put something in my spirit that was surprising to me. He was telling me to put down them cigarettes and come out from amongst them. And then

He(God) spoke to me saying, start changing your ways because I'm not going to have you shame My name with all the reading and going to church and then coming back smoking cigarettes and talking trash to the slicksters.

What really put icing on the cake was when God gave me an alternative, which really moved my attention. He told me if I come to a certain level in Him before my parole date, He will let me out. Now God knew how bad I wanted out, so He put this in front of me to run for. And believe it or not it was on, it was a personal thing between me and God. Every time I would do anything out of character, I was convicted down in my soul. My flesh was beginning to war with my spirit and it was like my flesh knew there was a change going on. There wasn't a soul there that knew what was going on, matter of fact, I didn't neither at the time. All I knew, I had company within myself and the more I was reading, the more convictions were going on. I kept striving and striving, trying to change. I felt myself fading away from the crowd more and more.

By this time, It was time for me to move out of this dorm and I believed God was putting me in a whole new environment. Oh yeah, before I was moved to this new environment, I went through or witnessed a great miracle, God created through me. I remembered speaking to God about me smoking cigarettes and was telling Him it was to hard to quit smoking. I told Him, I done tried several times and I would still fall back into the same trend. Then I thought I was putting Him on the spot when I said to Him, if you take away the taste out of my mouth, maybe I can quit. After I made that statement, days went by and I didn't think nothing else about it. But one day after I was done eating, I always needed a cigarette after I ate. And at this particular time a couple of hours went by and a friend of mine asked for a cigarette, which reminded me that I haven't had one. So I told him I'll be right back, I have some in my locker. Before I went back to my friend, I decided to take me a smoke while using the restroom. I pulled out a cigarette out of a new pack and started puffing on it but it was tasting nasty. I looked at it and threw it away thinking it was just a bad or old cigarette. Then I pulled out another one and it tasted nasty also. So now I looked at the pack and was thinking the pack was old. At that very moment, I realized what I had said to the Father earlier about taking the taste out of my mouth. Right then, I thought and looked at the pack and said to myself, God have took the taste out of my mouth so I might as well, quit fighting it. At that very moment, I got rid of my new pack of cigarettes. And my flesh would yearn for a cigarette from time to time but everytime I tried to smoke one, it would taste nasty, so I quit trying to fight against what God had granted me, which was deliverance.

My inner spirit was warring with the flesh with everything I was doing until the victory with the cigarettes. Then the Holy Spirit put in my mind, after forty years of doing wrong, why is it so hard to do right? Right then, I made up my mind to switch that thing by making it hard to do wrong and easy to do right. Then I allowed my inner spirit to have it's way in my life, to take over my flesh and that's what it done, took over. Immediately, I was walking in freedom. Now with this new transformation and new environment, It seemed like God was raising me to another level, in which He was. I came in the new dorm with a new will for my life and didn't realize it, at the time. Every step was like a calculated step which meant, everything was more visible and accounted for.

Walt and Dee were getting classes together to rehearse for our choir and Bible studies. And it seemed like the studies were getting more and more intensed, we were getting more and more serious and rooted in the Word. Dee would even asked me or Walt to lead devotion with prayer or scripture by surprise, he called it stepping out on faith. But we would tell him to let us know ahead of time so we could be prepared but he came with a comment, "be ye ready at all times". By this I commenced to study and prepare myself for these situations. The good part about this were, the more I was determined, the more the Holy Spirit moved in and really gave me the lesson I couldn't forget. The Holy Spirit put a burning desire down in me, whereas, I was wishing Dee called on me now. If he didn't, sometimes I'll volunteer.

From this point on, I started getting a deep passion for the Word. I ate every Word that proceeded out of the mouth of God. I examined every quotation, every saying, every religion and every sermon. I wouldn't let nothing go unnoticed, not even situations that was going on around me or people in their different personalities and hang-ups, God allowed me to notice everything. Day-in and day-out I sat in my room studying or listening to my Walkman about the Word. The only time I departed from the Word was when I went to eat or came up for a breather. Even then, I went right back to it not wanting to depart from it, one minute. At this time, I didn't know what was happening, all I knew, I was getting hooked on the Word and loving every minute of it. But while I was getting a deeper and deeper relationship with God, I didn't noticed, I was closing myself from my friends and fellow brethren. I stop playing horseshoes and basketball, two things I loved most. The Lord had me feeling like Apostle Paul, with my mind setting in the third heaven. Satan was giving me problems in the night while I was sleeping. He was desiring me to misuse my body for his purpose but God would step in and wake me up right on time. This happen a number of times but God was there every time interrupting satan's plan. It finally came to an halt and it was plain as day to me what was going on. I knew satan was attacking me in my sleep and I couldn't prevent it myself, but God. And after I was seldom seen for a while, the guys started coming in to where I was trying to get me to come outside. They would say, "boy you're getting serious with that stuff", come out and get some air. I did finally, started coming out but I felt like a bear that had been in hibernation for months. When I came out it was like I was another person. I didn't know then like I know now that I was under the Anointing.

God had step me up to higher level in His wisdom, His understanding and His knowledge. The Anointing was like a shield that shielded off any fiery darts that came my way. Everywhere I went on the yard was like it was just me and God walking and talking quietly to each other, no matter how many people were around. It was like I was behind a curtain, where I could see everything going on but they couldn't touch me physically or mentally, it was the greatest feeling I've ever felt. One morning I got up and seen one of my brethren in Christ torn in pieces. He kept repeating the devil, the devil is all around, all of them are devils, pointing to different people. He was in turmoil, highly upset when I came up, so I tried to calm him down. I told him quit promoting the devil and promote Jesus Christ. I told him, I feel so full of Jesus Christ I almost forgot about the devil exist. I said satan who? Who is satan? My mind was to wrapped up in Jesus. And he begun to calm down and came back to himself, where we could fellowship in peace.

As time went on, the brethrens of the choir kept rehearsing and singing for the Lord. Between rehearsals we continued to have Bible Studies, some guys agreed and some didn't. The ones that didn't later dropped out because they wanted to sing more than they wanted to see God. But one thing for sure, the three of us remained through thick and thin, Walt, Dee and I. We stayed committed to the cause. Guys on the yard criticized our singing and even formed their own group thinking of themselves as professional singers compared to us. They competed with us but were quickly resolved because of their cause. We picked up a very good lead singer from the group who was sincere in what he was doing. So we voted him in and things were beginning to change because the new guy was putting everybody's voice where it was supposed to be. The more we sung at church, the more guys was coming to hear us sing. Through the Blessing of God, He orchestrated a choir that was pleasing to the ears. And in spite of the jealousy, these same people came and packed the church to hear us sing.

We continued studying and coming closer to the Lord until one day the Supervisor of the kitchen took some cooks with her which two of them were

Walt and Dee. They came back with a truck full of snacks, merchandise and other stuff we weren't supposed to have on the yard. Everybody in the kitchen were excited and in a uproar because of getting stuff we couldn't have. Even I was excited of trying to get my share and then some more. Then the Holy Spirit convicted me badly of getting caught up in worldly stuff. So I started backing up and started observing more, but the stuff were very tempting and because of this it was hard to resist. The Holy Spirit kept speaking to my mind, telling me to back off, so gradually I stopped looking for stuff and started focusing on God. Unfortunately though, my brethren in Christ, Walt and Dee were very excited of the merchandise and continued to receive it. Conflicts were brewing up from the other guys toward Walter and Dee, complaining about the amounts they were getting. But Walt and Dee repeatedly announced, this was a blessing from God and they were going to receive much as they could and then some more. They done just what they said and problems kept occurring between the guys and Walt and Dee. Nevertheless, Walt and Dee continued to hold their grounds.

Some of the guys were trying to get me upset at them by asking me, what have they done for you lately? You suppose to be their right hand man but yet they hand you out baby size stuff, if that. Satan was stirring around in the midst, through material stuff but I stayed steadfast in my studying and was allowing the Holy Spirit to make my every move. And the Holy Spirit revealed to me something strange from this incident about Walt and Dee. But I couldn't just put my finger on it at the time. And on down the road, God did show me and you'll pick it up to, just keep on reading. One thing for sure, the stuff they had, brought on a lot of distractions. By no surprise, one morning the correctional officers had a lock down and demanded for full inspection. They went through the whole yard in no time, throwing away anything that wasn't supposed to be there. Walter and Dee suffered a great loss with their material stuff. And believe it or not, I noticed a slight change in their altitude, which was good. God desires us to stay focus on His will and purpose for our lives. We are to stay fine tuned to His voice so we don't get swept away in life and from the things of life.

Time was getting close for my parole date and I knew God wanted me to reach a certain level of obedience before I went in front of the board. So I continued to allow my flesh to die so that the Holy Spirit could change me and mold me to who I suppose to be. It wasn't easy, matter of fact, my biggest test came from the kitchen, when I was working and one of my friends I practical grew up with cursed me out for not stealing him something he wanted very badly. He repeatedly asked me because I had done it before but now it was different. Now I was operated under the Holy Spirit and I already knew I was being convicted on everything I was doing. After he seen that I wasn't feeling it, he looked at me with one of the nastiest looks and told me, I'm nothing and cursed me out and told me, don't ever come around him again. The Holy Spirit revealed to me right then, how your friends will flip on you for trying to do what's right. But regardless, I was proud of myself for not yielding to my flesh. Finally, it was time for my parole day and yes I was scared but happy. I was happy because I had faith that I had reached the level of obedience God was looking for. So deep down in my soul I felt like going home.

We all from the camp, loaded up to take the ride to the place where the parole hearing was being held. We gathered in a big cafeteria with inmates from all over the county. The group I came with, all mostly sit together and our families sat on the other side of the room. My mother, sisters and girlfriend were there and I was still nervous. All of the guys that was sitting at my table were speaking negative toward the hearing. But I was very careful not to mention a word. Even when they asked me my opinion, I was still quiet because I knew in this length of time of my walk in God, you can't mix faith and negativity. I sit there in anticipation and in wonder, thinking maybe my will is not God's will for me to go home. I even made myself feel comfortable by accepting the fact that if God wanted me to stay behind the wall to profess His Word, I would. I was scared but not of lack of faith because I knew without a shout of a doubt God had delivered me and from this I was willing to go where ever He sent me or do whatever He wanted me to do. But the desire of my heart was to go home and be with my family. So when they called me for my turn, I walked in with confidence, knowing that either way, God was going to use me no matter what. The Board asked me questions and I answered them, they spoke with my mother and family about me. Then they made a decision and told me I made it. I jumped for joy and hugged and kissed everybody, I was ready and anxious to go right then. But unfortunately, we had to go back to the yard.

Days passed by after I made parole and I was trying to be as patient as I could but I was beginning to worry, wondering what in the world is going on. I went up to the front to operations to find out what was the hold up. They told me that it was something on my record keeping me in, so I immediately went to called my mother to find out what was going on and to have something done about it quickly. Two weeks had went by and it was going on the third and furthermore, it was getting close to the holidays in November and December. Once you get caught up during that time you can hang it up, you'll in for a long stay. I was upset and running to the phone every day but I thank God for the brethren, because Walt helped me eased my anxiety and convinced me to settle down and concentrate on what God is doing. So I got back into the rhythm of praising and worshipping and witnessing. I had confidence that my mother was taking care of business on the outside. Another week went by and I was sitting in the courtyard on a bench, when I noticed guys going to rehabilitation, which furnished shoes, clothes and work material. I thought, if I could get in on it, maybe I can get me some extra stuff but it was a guy sitting next to me, speaking in a small voice telling me he had been watching me and seen the change in me. Then he reminded me of how good God have been to me and all I have to do is trust Him. During these few weeks of waiting to be released, I realized two things God brought to my spirit and that was to be patient and trust Him fully. I was getting ready to face the world and all of the temptations of life. Even though, I felt the Anointing and was filled with the Holy Spirit, I was still afraid.

TEMPTATION

It was finally my chance to go home, my mother had taken care of all the problems that was holding me up. I was very excited about getting back into society once again. But my only hang up was that I didn't know how I would do with my new life as a christian. I really had second thoughts because this time I really loved the Lord for who He is, and my spirit had connected with the Holy Spirit and it was a difference. My first challenge was my girlfriend, who I knew would be hard to resist. I had subjected my body and mind to Christ to do right in everything I did. But now I was facing the biggest challenge with my girlfriend. Making love was easy before for me because I wasn't a christian, even though she was. Now I could understand her feelings toward God in doing the wrong thing in His sight.

On my release day, they called me to operations and my girlfriend was standing there waiting to pick me up. She looked so gorgeous and immediately I had to check myself. We were so excited about seeing each other, we gave each other the biggest hug ever. We embraced each other like we hadn't seen each other in years and those nine months certainly seemed like years. Even in the embracing, right then I felt the fire out of our bones and flesh like I never felt before, and I'm sure she felt the same thing because we jumped back as if we committed a sin. While leaving the place, the air felt so different, so fresh on the other side of the fence. Even though, both sides were outdoors, it just seemed like the air behind the fence was much heavier, gloomier and stuffier. While the air on this side seemed like a burden had been lifted, everything felt much lighter and cleaner. And you know, walking out of there a true born again believer, versus when I first came in, a confused, lost soul, is very much the same as the "lighter air". My spirit was a joyful, unconfused and an assured man of God. My mind, soul and heart were convinced who I was, because now I loved the Lord Jesus more than anything in the world. It wasn't a put on or an impression to prove to people I had changed. No sir, this was real this time, this was a personal thing me and the Lord had together. He opened my eyes and enlightened my understanding of who I am in Christ and what I was up against. My Father in Heaven had let me know that it wasn't my family or the people or anybody else I was going up against, it was me and satan. Once God showed me who and what I had to destroy in me, then satan wasn't so bad.

Because of who I thought I was and what I was working with was an open door for satan. Many times, I had came over on this side with lack of understanding, thinking I was going to save somebody, when in reality I wasn't saved yet myself. So many of us jump out into the ministry too fast, not finding out who we really are in Christ eyes and not knowing what He really want out of our lives. A lot of people jump out in the ministry with messed up ways, with attitudes wrapped inside, stubborn ways and not seeing it and last but not lease, impressions, trying to impress or please people to get credibility and position from them. It's our nature, everything I mentioned are natural for all of us, we all like to be glorified in some form or fashion. But Jesus prayed at Gethsamethe that this cup pass over Him because of the pain and suffering He seen ahead. Then He goes on to say, nevertheless, let your will be done that the Father be glorified and with You being glorified then I will be glorified also. So you see, God knows our nature, He made us. What He ask is that we glorify Him with all our heart, with all our soul and with all our mind. In doing this, God will glorify you, then you want need glorification from man. But just like Jesus had to endure some pain and suffering, so are we if we are to be called truly, children of God. The most pain and suffering we'll have to endure is denying ourselves and allowing the Holy Spirit to change and mold us in who He wants us to be. And for all of us it is painful, destroying the old Temple to build a new Temple, refine as gold. Those who think nothing is wrong with them, I feel sorry for them because they'll never walk into the full anointing God has for them until they tear down that old Temple (the soul).

Getting back to walking out of the prison with my girlfriend, I knew I had to keep my distance from her. My Lord was really close to me now, so I really felt bad even thinking about doing something wrong. But my flesh had another thought of it's own and it was getting stronger, the more I thought about it. So here I was now, after God had molded me and changed me from a lot of bad habits and temptations that I had in jail, now I'm faced with a whole new set of temptations, the world and everything in it. We stopped very close to get something to eat, then we rode thirty minutes back to Greenville making our first stop at her house. She knew what time it was as well as I did, neither one of us could resist any longer. Our flesh was burning with desire for one another. And to keep from beating around the bush, we made love like we never made before, simply because we had missed each other so much.

But little that she knew, I had established a different kind of love from her, when she gave me all of her love while I was locked up. She showed me so much love that it was built up in my heart to love again. She gave the kind of love a mother gives to her child even though he had strayed away, she still loved him a million times over. The same is with God, He loves us over and over again, even though we don't deserve it or appreciate it. He still shows unconditional love. Even in the Old Testament, God constantly reminded Israel to obey His commandments but they continued falling to the wayside. God would get angry and issue out punishment but He said in His Word in Isaiah 9:12, for all this, His anger is not turned away, but His hand is stretched out still. My girlfriend and I were getting very comfortable seeing each other on a regular basis as if we had pushed God aside, until the Holy Spirit stepped in and started convicting us. We were harshly convicted in our soul, so we decided to stop because we knew we were sinning in God eyes. We both of course, repented to God.

I started back getting adjusted to things around me again, getting rid of things I no longer needed. The courts had ordered me to go to these drug classes once a month and also report to my parole officer. After my girlfriend and I slowed up seeing each other, I began to study and get more consecrated in the Lord. I wanted to feel that closeness and burning urgency I felt when I was in jail. It was a burning that took me to higher heights in the Lord. And that's what I wanted to do, go up higher in the Lord. So I started listening to programs on television and on the radio of everything concerning Gospel. I was reading for long periods of time and I was trying to catch every church service in town. Not just with my church but with every church that was having the move of God. I was excited about the insight God had showed me about Himself. I wanted people to know my testimony and my love for God the Father. I was very bold about what I knew about God. I was going into church services bold and free, and the churches were thinking I was coming to join but in my heart we were already joined. The truth was like a two-edge sword in my mouth and a buried treasure in my heart waiting to be found.

I remembered the first day of my drug class, the teacher had everybody pronounce their names and behind it, he wanted us to admit we were reformed drug addicts. Then we were to say, we couldn't go back to the same areas again and expect to stay clean. This was well and good but when it came to my turn I couldn't do it. The teacher of the class asked why and suggested that we had to say it to help us know who we are or were. But I told him and the whole class, I was not a reformed drug addict but a child of God. Then I went on to tell him once God clean you up, you're clean from all unrighteousness, so if I'm cleaned in God's eyes, then I'm cleaned. This being my first time in a drug class, I didn't know reformed nearly meant the same thing, I just didn't like reminding myself or speaking out over and over again of what I was. Furthermore, I asked him, how do you all expect us to stay out of our old situations when we get out of jail, when there are no doors to go through to help us keep from going backwards and you all are not trying to make it better. The teacher looked at me surprised, and said, you're right, I think I'll try to look into this and see if I can get someone in here to help with extra schooling and maybe help with jobs also.

In the meantime he said, I'm having a former pastor coming in to talk with you all. Then when the former pastor came in, he came in fired up as if he already knew what was going on. The Holy Spirit was all over me like a covered anointing of truth. Every word that came out of my mouth was as if it wasn't me. It was like I was possessed by some force that was controlling my thinking and words. It was something wonderful because it had the students in class at "awe" and the teacher and former pastor were amazed, wondering where was I getting such words and boldness. It threw the former pastor off balance so much that he started talking delirious, laughing, using profanity, which made me wonder, what kind of pastor would use profanity. But anyway, the class finally finished and everybody went their separate ways. My parole was still going on, I think I had a year to go.

During this time, I had went to this Temporary Company, seeking a job. Before I got locked up, I worked for them from time to time and immediately they had a job for me on the same day. I was really happy to have a job even though it was hard. I needed money for support not only for myself but for my daughter also, plus I had to give my mother some money for living in her house. She wasn't pressuring me or nothing but I knew I just couldn't live off her. She was already doing everything for me anyway, including taking and picking me up from work. I was just in a mess, which I had caused on my own. Nevertheless, I continued to press on, standing on the Word. The knowledge of the Word kept me and sustained me and I stood on it. I wished I would have known this Word a long time ago. I don't believe I would have been in this predicament.

But little that I knew, tests were headed my way that I wasn't aware of. At this time in my life, I was praying night and day, meditating regularly. One verse in particularly, I was praying daily for, "Let me deny myself and pick up the Cross and follow You(Jesus)". And sure enough, that was exactly what was happening in my life. The Holy Spirit could had been prompting me to pray this verse. Because just like Jesus endured the struggle of the Cross, now

I was about to also. My Temporary Company called me in for an update on my application, which I thought was fine. I filled it out until I got down to the part where they asked, have I ever been convicted of a felony? It stunned me for a while and I had to think if I should put yes or no. Before I went to jail I would have said no, but because I was now living the truth, I was convicted to tell the truth. Plus, the small print said your employment will not be effected. So with faith I put yes and was hoping they would accept it. I gave the application to the lady and she said, "oh you have a felony" and I tried to explain but she quickly shut me up and told me they couldn't use me anymore, that the job was finished. I mentioned the underline words in small print but she said it didn't matter, they can't use me. I went out sad and gloomy thinking how I was cut down just by telling the truth. Then I was reminded of the scripture, which said the saints will be persecuted for righteousness sake.

I went home in turmoil, wondering what am I going to do. I paced the floor knowing I needed a job. I was getting angry at the world and at myself for being in this predicament. At home with mom at forty-one years old, without a license because of my driving record and plus trying to raise a daughter, brought on self pity. Satan was moving in quickly, but thank God for the Word because immediately I started rebuking satan and calling him a liar and telling him the truth is not in him. I told the Lord I was His child and I know He is suppose to take care of His children. Then I said to myself, I'm not lying down on this one. I stood on the Word of God for strength and wisdom and right then the Holy Spirit brought to my attention, about this certain guy who worked there in the same place as a Supervisor and was a friend of mine from way back. I called the Plant for him and got his answering service. Even then, I felt confident that things were beginning to get into motion. I waited until the next day and called again and finally, I reached him and told him my situation. He gave me instructions on what to do and I was back on the job the next day, praise the Lord. The work was hard but it was good to have at this time. I really made it worth while when I was able to witness every chance I got. I didn't go around bothering anybody because I mostly stayed to myself. But as I constantly read the word and studied every chance I had, it kind of drew people to curiosity which made them asked questions. This would give me a chance to really witness, which I had gained a passion for. Simple reason, because God had revealed Himself to me so much, I couldn't keep it all to myself, I had to tell it to someone.

We had a hard nose Leadsman on this job, who had no sympathy. He didn't smile or speak unless you made him speak. Everybody in our five man crew were terrified of him. But for some reason I just couldn't be, he was just an ordinary man who needed to know what love was. It seemed like he resented me more and more because I didn't jump like everybody else. I respected him but I had learned from the Holy Spirit to fear no man but fear God. One of the guys came in a little before I did as a Temp and was giving out smart remarks about competing with me for the job. He spoke to me about the Bible also, letting me know he knew enough to make it. I tried to quote scripture to him and tell him about some real life issues, trying to get him to see things at another point of view. But I guess, he had his mind made up and friction was beginning to arouse. This was a test coming and I couldn't see it or I refused to see it. Anyway, the guy had got hired on and he boasted about having a job and I didn't. One day, I told him to come out of that slave mentality, he got furious and ran to the office to tell on me. The Leadsman stopped me and had words with me. After that I couldn't believe he told on me so I got upset and we ended up in the locker room after work, mouthing at each other. This was a great opportunity for satan to move in. I went as far as calling him a sissy and punk for running up front. The heat aroused even more, now I was on the edge standing over him with satan in my mind telling me to hit him and telling me you know you don't take nothing like this. Then the Holy Spirit reminded me of who I am. Then after I wouldn't hit him, satan spoke to my mind to curse him out, which the whole time I hadn't used any profanity. Yet I was still fired up and felt like cursing him but the Holy Spirit wouldn't let me curse him. The Lord gave me enough Grace not to go completely over the edge. After that day I never stepped foot in that place again. The Temp place called me to tell me they no longer needed me. Now I was out of a job again but I was able to get an unemployment check. Still, I couldn't wait on an unemployment check, I had the desire to work. I had that desire to keep moving further than where I was.

I surely thanked God for the Old Testament. I read it all the way through and the Holy Spirit revealed a lot of what God liked and what He disliked. He showed me how He kept His people moving from one place to another until they reached the Promise Land and had the true faith. Through all His revelation, I knew in my heart what would kindle His anger and what would kindle His Love. And by this, I knew God had a purpose for me and it was up to me to follow His instructions to find out exactly what it was He wanted me to do. I had come from one stage to another. By saying this, while I was locked up in jail God showed me a written word about a wandering lamb that kept wandering away from the flock and the shepherd would go out and find that lamb, then break his legs and mend them back together, then carry him on his shoulder so the lamb could get used to staying with the flock while he healed. That's the way God done me, He broke me up, sat me down in a place, where I had to learn how to walk with the flock. Now I can say, I loved every minute of what He did. The second stage was when I got out of jail, I felt like a baby eagle after he had finally been weaned from his mother and his wings had reached it's length before his first flight. The baby eagle takes off by God's Grace not knowing how long he will fly or where he flies. But with confidence and faith he flies with Grace all over the land. That day I was released, I felt like my wings had opened and I didn't know where I was going or how long I was going for. One thing I did know with faith and confidence, through God's Grace I will fly with great strength, with new wings and great wisdom of God's will. Thank God for His grace and mercy and the strength of His Word, which kept me and is still keeping me. Temptations never stops but life goes on

LIFE GOES ON

The last job I was on, I found a brochure about going to a community college. The first thing that came to my mind was to apply for a management position. So while I wasn't working I checked into it and pursued it. First of all, I had to get a grant or a federal loan, so I filled out the necessary applications and they sent me back a letter of denial because of the felony I had. But I wouldn't stop there, I tried again and even got on the phone with some guy who worked with the Federal Loan place. He patiently heard my situation and decided to give me a break. He told me not to worry, he'll take care of it. Everything went through for me to enter in the school. My first week in school was very interested and I liked it very much. I met some very interesting people there, one in particular was a guy who asked me what was my religion and I told him I had no denomination. I asked him what was his religion and he told me he was a Wesylyn Methodist and something else, which I couldn't understand. I told him, "I don't know what all that were, but I do know one thing, as long as you believe in Jesus Christ you are alright with me". After our discussion, I realized I was in a Bible College, which was good.

I was getting my mother to drop me off there, as she was doing everywhere I was going. Sometimes the school would get into projects that required groups to meet and study in other locations, but at times I wasn't able to meet because of lack of transportation. I walked to school at times because I was determined to do something I never done before. I was there for a month, when a friend came by the house with another friend who was telling me about this job he was on. I asked him could he get me on some kind of way and immediately I was hired for a third shift job. It was a twelve hour shift, working two days on and two days off. I needed a job badly but it enabled me to go to school so now I was stuck in the middle of a choice between school and work. God knew I needed a job but I wanted a career from going to school. I tried to arrange suitable hours from school to meet with my schedule at work, but the people from school couldn't make any adjustments. One night while at work, I was reading a book from school when the Holy Spirit spoke to me on what I was reading and told me this material I'm reading was very much like the Word or Bible I've been teaching you all a long. Then the Holy Spirit told me if I drop this school and continue learning from Him, I'll have even better wisdom. He also told me He'll teach me to be a better manager. The next day I went to the college and resigned and turned in all my paperwork and books and said goodbye. I was excited because I knew, when the Holy Spirit told me this, I was going toward a great adventure.

The work was real slow and easy, so during the slack times I stayed buried in the Word. The Holy Spirit was right, the Word was giving me great knowledge and revealing great revelation and mysteries from the Old and New Testament. The only thing I would miss was the degree I was going after. On this job I was a helper to an operator who was straight up prejudice. A rebel flag talking and wearing guy. But I tried not to let him bother me because I came in doing the service of the Lord. I would work so much and so diligently, some would come to tell me not to work like that, I told them I just couldn't help it, I had to keep my mind occupied. I continued working and reading the Word every chance I got. The Operator showed me what he wanted me to know and nothing else. He withheld a lot of important things concerning the job from me. But at this time it didn't matter, I just stayed diligent on what I did know. The Operator could see how much I was in the Word, so now he wanted to see how much I loved the Word. He started pushing buttons that would offend me or make me angry but I refused to drop down to his level. I was full of the Holy Spirit which kept me on my toes. I seen through him so clearly, when he came at me the wrong way as to provoke me, I gently died in Christ each time. In otherwords, my flesh died and Christ in me rose and I tolerated it with no problem. In doing this it kept him off balance, even though he still would continue to come at me in rude actions, because this had been his nature for a long time. Some times our nature becomes a habit to us rather if it's good or bad. Each time he came to me, I would die in Christ in order to be raised in Christ. This didn't make me lesser of a man but a bigger man. And God made me see this clearly, when my operator started coming to me for counseling and asking me what kind of literature I had for him to read. At times he asked me far out questions about God's creations. That's why I thank God for His revelations and great mysteries He gave me because now I was able to answer some of these far out questions he was asking me. See it's not only good to read God's Word, but also asking God to reveal to you His great revelations and great mysteries of His Word. There's more in His scriptures than we ever can comprehend on our own. God had restored my mental senses again, gave me integrity and made me a new man.

Now God was beginning to restore material things to me and first it was my driving license. It was one of the most amazing experiences of my life. I had $1700 dollars of reinstatement fees and charges against me. I went a few times trying to see how I could get my driving license and to me it seemed impossible. Plus, one of the ladies behind the desk told me, I had a judgment against me at the courthouse causing me not to get my license. So I went there to see what it was, already knowing that I was in a hit and run accident and went to jail for it, so I was thinking it might be still pending on me from an insurance company. But as I searched the computer with the clerk of court, she told me she didn't see any judgment concerning my license and I gave a "sigh" of relief. But she went on to say, there were other judgments against me though, from losing my house to owing the Federal Revenue and amongst other things. I left that courthouse in despair, walking and thinking to myself what terrible shape I was in. I said, God You seen what was on my record and I'm not doubting You because Your Word says it's nothing impossible for You, but this is a mess and I'll leave it like that. Now the lady at the courthouse had already told me, there wasn't anything against my license, I should've been celebrating that. After going and not accomplishing anything, I had gave up on getting them right then. Then the Holy Spirit told me to go and try again. I had the nerve to asked the Holy Spirit, "are You sure about this"? Then I said to Him, I've tried twice already and You're telling me to try again. So I done just as the Holy Spirit requested. Satan was trying to remind me of the courthouse experience of my situation being hopeless and telling me I'll never own anything again. But I told him, he is a liar and the truth is not in him. I continued doing what the Holy Spirit was telling me to do. And I thanked God, I got my hands on the money $1700 dollars exactly without owing anybody.

I went back to the driver license place and a young lady pointed me out to this certain lady behind the desk. This certain lady looked over my situation and was determined to help me as if she was appointed. Even though, I didn't have the money with me, she told me to come back tomorrow to her window and see her only. The next day I went back to the highway department and it was over crowded. Her line were out the door and I said to myself, oh lord, she said see her only. So I patiently paused and obeyed her instructions, I stuck my face in the door to allow her to see me in her presence. And immediately she said come on and let me take care of you. Looking at the long line, I done exactly what she said and not only was I pushed up ahead of the line but she arranged for me to get my license without taking the test over. Within thirty minutes I was out of there with my license. God had showed me another miraculous thing that day on what He can do.

I had been on this job for a year and people was coming and going. One of the christian friends I had in jail name Walt was still keeping in contact with me. He introduced me to his girlfriend and wife to be, who he met while in jail. He always said God sent her to him and I believed it too. He wasn't working so I tried to help him by giving him some money, when he asked, until he got a job. I was giving him good money at times and it seemed like the more I gave the more he wanted. But being a brother in Christ I didn't mind. A thought came over my mind at one time, thinking he was getting money for drugs because I had been in the drug game before so I knew the symptoms. But I didn't want to think of the worst scenario so I brushed it off, but from this I did learned one thing and that was not to get in the way of God. I gave to him because I loved him in a godly way but love goes further than just giving a person everything they want, sometimes you have to say no.

Finally I was able to convince my supervisor to hire him. Walt worked real well the first few weeks, I was training him and showing him everything I knew. I was very zealous of talking about the Lord, I would get chill bumps from excitement when talking about the Lord's Word. Walt and I shared some deep revelations together. But gradually, he started fading away from sharing the Lord's Word with me. He started sleeping on the job and talking that street talk to me, like he was on the block. He was talking with his girlfriend by phone, long periods of times while on the job. I was constantly speaking to Walt to correct his actions with the Holy Spirit leading me. I even told Walt he was concentrating on his girlfriend more than God's Word. He laughed and took everything I was saying as a joke. Now this was the same guy who was a fellow worshipper in prison with me. He spoke in tongue and was filled with the Holy Spirit. But he was one of the guys who God gave me revelation about concerning their weakness while in jail, in which I couldn't grasped at the time. I started asking him questions about the Holy Spirit. One of the questions were, if a person was in the Spirit is it possible he could be fading away from the Spirit and not know it? He answered me straight up, saying once a person is filled with the Holy Spirit he can't fade away. So I stopped with the questions and told him that the Holy Spirit wouldn't have him acting the way he was acting. He wanted to argue the point but I left it like it was and didn't want to go any further with it. I was feeling bad about the way he was acting on the job, the Spirit in me was quenched. I was realizing more and more he was falling away from Grace.

I went to a scripture in the Bible to try to convince Walt to get back on track. The Holy Spirit gave me Deuteronomy 30:16-21 to give to him. I read it and showed it to him. I even explained it to him so he could fully understand it. The girl he said, God sent to him was probably true but I told him if you don't be obedient to God's Word at the best you can be or if you deliberately disobey His Word without repentance, God will forfeit His promise to you. I told him this and I believed it with all of my heart. God told Moses to tell His people when they get over into the Promise Land He gave them and forget who gave it to them or get the big head and boast on themselves as if they done it. God told Moses I will surely take it back. So I told Walt, he won't have me taking care of him in a little while and I was getting ready to exit out of his presence. I told him, you won't have me picking you up and taking care of you on this job all the time, so you better start now, getting focus on what you are doing. Right then, I spoke a prophecy and didn't know it. That next night we were beginning to start work and he came to me crying and hurt, so we went to privacy and he admitted that he had been doing wrong in God's sight and he was hurt about it. Then he admitted, all the times he received money from me he bought drugs with it. He told me he was on drugs all this time and he just couldn't live a lie any longer. We prayed and I cried along with him feeling the pain deeply. And not to say that I was surprised and disappointed because of all the times I gave him money to help him and he was buying drugs with it. I had bent over backwards helping him and he done me like this. But I still refused to let satan get in this so I had sympathy and prayed strongly for his recovery.

I told him he need to leave his neighborhood because it constantly reminded him of something he left behind. It was a trap for him to see all the familiar surroundings that he was trying to destroy out of his life. I told him about the story of why sheep have hooves, so they could flee to the rocks when in danger of a wolf because wolves couldn't climb rocks like sheep. I told him this, so he could consider moving to higher grounds. He listened and was excited about it so he made arrangements to move to a place for homeless and regenerating people, which was forty miles away from his town and neighborhood. But before he moved, I had quit the job we were on, leaving him there. I heard he was fired and moved away to the place for help.

I had gotten me a car now so I thought I could do better than this job I was on. I went and applied with a company because it was a much better job, with more pay. The only thing about this job, it had stipulations in which I heard about, before I went there. It consisted of criminal background checks, I thought I could beat it, like others did. I told them about my record in bits and pieces. I wanted a good job again so bad that I took a chance and left my old job without thinking or praying to my God. The Holy Spirit had been leading me all this time, except for this particular time when I pushed the Holy Spirit aside and done my on thing without even checking with Him. Anyway, I worked there about three weeks or more and the leadsman and the supervisor were pleased with my work. They were talking about hiring me until a report came in about my criminal record. They called me in the office and told me I was terminated. This was a bad day for me, I was intensed, wondering what am I going to do now? I went back to my little room at my mothers house, where I still lived and commenced seeking the Lord trying to find out what to do now. I repented and confessed the mistake I made for moving ahead of the Holy Spirit. I asked God to renew my spirit and give me the will to do His will even more stronger than before.

I really thanked God for T. D. Jakes, Noel Jones, Anita Bynum, Marvin Winans, Joyce Myers, and William L. Bonner and plus many more for their continuing ministries from the Lord. Staying lined up with the Holy Spirit and bringing His right now Word. They really kept me focus and whenever I fell, they were right their in the Spirit picking me back up with their messages from the Lord. I had to come under subjection to the Holy Spirit in order to get back lined up with Him. Even though God knows our weaknesses, we still need to submit to the Holy Spirit to be fine tuned to His Will. I felt confident that God heard my cry and was going to deliver me from my own mess.

So I went on the search for another job. I looked high and low, calling old and new connections. And in doing this God was still showing me the "Path Of Life". This particular day I called "the crossroads of my life", one of the strangest things happen. When I was riding across town worrying about my situation of being without a job, I came to this red light. It was full of traffic with a eighteen wheel truck to my left and cars and construction to my right. As I was sitting there thinking about myself changing jobs and now confused and needing a Word from the Lord, all of a sudden a chipmunk was crossing the road. As he was crossing, he went by my car and stopped under the trailer truck and looked around like he was confused. So I assumed that the construction over to my right had ran the chipmunk from his home. So the chipmunk was on the move not knowing where he was going. In spite of the dangerous highway, he paused and looked around and finally he proceeded on across the highway. It was a blessing, the traffic had come to a standstill. Once the chipmunk had gotten across the highway, he paused again in the business parking lot. As if he was thanking God for letting him make it across that busy highway and getting away from that loud, disturbing construction. Finally he was on the move again and he ran in these people yard, I guess to start another life or to make another home. But as I watched him, I thought about how scared we are sometimes to make a change, even when we are forced. If God will look after a chipmunk, He certainly will look after us. Then the light changed and I went on my way with confidence and faith.

Then one day a Temporary company called me for a job. It was forty to fifty miles away and the pay wasn't that good but regardless I took the job anyway. And I was faithful for the job by being there every day and on time. At first I knew this job was just for a moment until a month rolled around and then I was beginning to think of a possibility of getting hired. Then a revelation came over me one day at this little job in this little town. I had been doing as I usually do on my breaks and that's reading the Word. As I had stayed on the job for a few months, I had started witnessing to a few people, not by choice but because God drew these people to me. Then I realized God put an unction in my spirit to really witness to a few particular people on this job. I don't know why I was witnessing so strongly to these people but I done as God instructed me to do. Then God gave me a revelation and prophecy of the job so strongly that I didn't know how to tell it. All of a sudden, changes were beginning to happen, the same changes God had already put in my spirit. Right when we thought everything were progressing in our behalf, people started leaving mysteriously, disappearing right out from under our nose. So God spoke to my spirit to warn people what was happening, especially the ones I had been witnessing to so strongly. So I told them to make a change immediately because our job were getting ready to end. But it was to late, after that day everybody on our shift were laid off except me.

I was changed to another shift and while on this shift I was beginning to know a whole new group. And fortunately, I was able to witness to some of them in a round about way. There was one guy in particular, a Leadsman, who was very head strong, a power surged young man fresh out of college. He thought strongly about getting to the top no matter who he stepped on. He told me he didn't like me because I talked too much. Some people can't take the facts or I call it the truth. But anyway, as I was in the Spirit, I also told him the job was about to end. He told me no way, and said he didn't believe what I was saying. He simply said, I wasn't qualified to know anything about the job. He might have been right, I might not have known what he knowed about the job. But nevertheless, I did know what the Holy Spirit was putting in my spirit. This was the last time we talked because the Company laid off the whole department including the young man of so much power. There was no one there but a few, cleaning up and moving things out. I was one of these few people cleaning up and I searched the plant for this young man but never seen him again. This story brought to my mind thoughts of the

End Times. When we are warned and no one heeds to the warnings, where will we be? will we be lost? or will we be found?

From this time on, I was beginning to see clearer now. Moving from place to place was like a journey God had me on. I believe when God is working something in you and you are committing your whole heart with all your might and submitting to the Holy Spirit with truth, God will take you from place to place, showing Christ through you and at the same time molding and shaping you to be better. Reading in Genesis about Abraham, I always wondered why he was promised the Caanan Land and kept going around in the same circles, from place to place meeting different and sometimes the same people. Then the Holy Spirit revealed to me how God was molding, shaping and gaining trust and faith from him through these experiences. God opened my eyes even more by letting me know I was on this journey now for Him. It wasn't about me anymore, but for Him.

Time was going on and I was without a job again. I had idle time on my hands so I studied hard reading the Bible and listening to Gospel tapes I had recorded off television. I would get up early in the morning about 5:30AM to catch certain preachers. One of them was Bishop Anthony Jinwright and after him Bishop T.D. Jakes, then on Wednesdays' I watched Bishop Noel Jones. And Joyce Meyers was one of my favorites too, especially with the book "Battlefield Of The Mind". I really learned a lot from that book but by listening to them all, it really gave me an insight on a lot of important things about life and the Spirit. I couldn't afford to order their tapes so I recorded them. I said, whenever I get in shape, I will give them some money because they really helped me out spiritually. Even though, I knew they were worth more than money because they are so special to the ministry. They boosted the Ministry up to another level and by hearing them preach, they took me to another level more faster, thanks to the Lord. From day one, since I've been delivered I've took notes on top of notes. I listened to all sorts of preachers, some who preached damnation and judgment to some who preached love and money. All of the hearing and learning of different ministries, God engraved it on my heart. And after God put me on this higher level from His Word being preached, I really stop taking notes unless it was something I wanted to dig into, later. I believed I was beginning to reach God in a whole new prospective. I believed we had formed a closeness and relationship like living in the same household. I didn't have to write notes anymore because every word that I heard or read was engraved on my heart and mind. I believed I had became a part of God face to face. At this level I was praising God harder, worshipping more and giving revelations, God had revealed to me.

The church I was going to, which was my family church didn't know what to think because they seen me before and after. Some of the guys in church had my spirit quenched. I often wondered why we as Christians worries or better yet criticizes other churches or other people on how they worship or praise God. I heard smart remarks like "oh he act like he done been to heaven and back already" or even say to each other as members "oh I know you're going to be a preacher" or "go ahead preacher". All of us should be trying to reach a place of maturity in God's will. God wants to take us higher and He want our growth to grow stronger. Let's speak with maturity through the Holy Spirit instead of ourselves. God said be slow to speak and quick to hear. Otherwords, think before we speak and know that God wants all of us to love Him, to know Him, to grow in Him and to come to a place of Holiness. So let's pray for one another to get there where He wants us to be. Jesus said in Luke 9:50 about the sectarian to His disciples, not to forbid anyone who does things in His name and that's what we shouldn't do. Jesus said, whoever is not against us is for us. Jesus said "us" to let you know we all are fighting for salvation and as many of us that are joined the better.

THE LIBERTY THAT CAUSES YOU TO COMPROMISE

Now it was the third year since I been out of jail, walking in my new delivery from God. I was still struggling in areas, I just couldn't control on my own. One in particular was me trying to have a relationship with my girlfriend without sex. This was the lady who stuck with me all through jail, the one who I met when I was in the world. She was filled with the Holy Spirit but somehow our strength falls when our fleshly desires are put to test. Don't tell me it can't happen to you. Now, I was able to identify with her the things she was telling me all along. But still, my will was weak and I would try to justify myself so I could get close to her. She told me over and over again, I couldn't continue doing this by justifying. I would tell her God know I love you, He know I'm weak and I need help. I would pursue her strongly and get her to give in and we would make mad love. Then in minutes or sometimes seconds afterwards we would be convicted and began asking God for forgiveness. This continued often in the same pattern so much, God would break it up Himself. The reason I say this is because we would get angry with each other and not speak to each other for a month at a time. Then we'll call ourselves getting back together and fooling ourselves by thinking we could see each other without going that far. Well, I was the one doing the convincing and she was the one who was declaring, "it won't work", because we are sinning in God's sight. I knew this but I just couldn't stay away from her. Deep as I was in the Lord, I still had a deep desire to be with her, not only sexually but as a companion also. I desired that companion relationship so bad, I had to be purged to eliminate that desire.

One of the big issues that stood between us were very critical. I hadn't been divorced from my wife, and because of this she kept it very secretive from the people of her church, when I was totally opposite. But regardless of my situation with my wife, in which we had been separated for twenty years, I was still hearing God speaking to me about this lady being my future wife and if I just could stay away from her in sexual immorality, He would make it possible. I told her the same thing God was putting on my heart, then she told me God hadn't told her nothing. I often wondered was this really a promise God was telling me or was this a lustful desired fantasy I was on? As of this day I still believe God had made this promise to me.

She constantly told me to go back to try to gain my wife back again as the Bible says. She always felt like she had to be the one who broke this thing up because she was in the ministry before me and knew more in depth. She surely had more understanding on the Word and the standards that go alone with it. I myself was one who came from the streets during the wildness of my life. I was use to plenty of freedom because I had refused to come under the law of authority. So I would argue with her over the morals and standards a person suppose to have. I remembered reading what Apostle Paul wrote about liberty, so I told her she needed to loosen up because she was judging the friends that I had. These were friends I had while I was in the streets, in which we were tight companions, even though, they were still dealing drugs. She once said before, there was no way for us to marry with me having friends like them. I told her one of them was seeking advice from me, since I was older and seeking God now. But in sense of it all, I was the one misjudging the order of liberty. Apostle Paul wrote in 5:13, for you brethren have been called to liberty; only do not use liberty as an opportunity for the flesh. And I had to learn this the hard way, but I'll explain it later in the chapter. Apostle Paul had a way of expressing himself in these unsearchable mysteries as though he had experienced some of it himself.

Sometimes in our relationships that we have with one another, I believe God uses them for an example to express our relationship with Him. For instance, God spoke in the book of Hosea about his wife, how she was doing Hosea badly. God used this story for an example on how His people were doing Him badly but He was still there with outstretched arms. So when my girlfriend and I had problems in our relationship, which were many times, they sometimes subconsciously make me think how we were doing God. We finally broke up again and both of us went back into deep meditation, this time a little deeper. We had come to a point, where we didn't talk to each other for a long period of time. So I had assumed that it was over this time.

Being single-minded again, gave me a boost to really prove to myself that she was wrong about having standards and morals to go by. I was asked by one of the females at work, was it alright to go to the nightclubs? She said as long as she behave herself it shouldn't be anything wrong with going to the nightclubs. I told her it was alright to go out to the Clubs as long as she didn't show out. At this time I was trying to come out my shell of separation from the people on my job. So I was putting myself in a compromising position and didn't even know it. They were already saying at work, I separated myself from them too much. After my girlfriend and I broke up, I was thinking I had the liberty to do things freely. I was free but still under God's Grace. God was beginning to allow me to go through some things in my freedom.

During this break up, I was in the middle of going home or going to her house. The Holy Spirit was telling me to go home but my mind was telling me to go to my girlfriend house. So I went with my mind, knowing all the time I was in disobedience. As soon as I got about three blocks from her house I ran right in the back of two young girls who had stopped to make a left turn. I crashed the car and total loss it. Their car was barely damaged. I was in shock and the girls were in worst shock. The firemen came first and were seeing after the girls. Then the EMS Paramedics came and put the girls on stretchers. I was getting really worried, more for myself than for them. They had told me they were alright when we first hit but the EMS carried it a little further, just in case. At that time, I thought I better call my girlfriend to be with me. She came and stayed with me the whole time the highway patrolman was there. I was thinking he was going to sock it to me but he just gave me a fifty dollar ticket to go to court. My girlfriend told me, this was a blessing, the highway patrolman gave you a big break. But now I was without a car again.

What surprised me the most was when the Holy Spirit reminded me one week prior to this accident, what I said. I stood up in a small church, where I went to Bible Study on Tuesdays and gave the little congregation my testimony. I was full of the Holy Spirit when I got in front of everyone. I told them I refuse to let satan steal my joy again, little that I knew, he must have been listening too. When I said this about satan I meant every word of it. Because at this time I was running into people in different places in their arrogant state of mind, threatening and raising their voices at me and I would smile and say kind words to them to put their minds in another state. So after the Holy Spirit reminded me of what was going on, I knew I was under an attack with the enemy. But at first, I had broken down in tears and was highly upset because of the setback. You see, God stepped back because of my disobedience to Him and allowed satan to touch me. But at this time, I couldn't see it or understand it so I asked God why did this have to happen? And after I was reminded, I wiped my tears from my face and spoke with boldness to satan. I told him, you are a liar and the truth is not in you. Then I got angry and told him, this is a personal thing now and I'm getting ready to praise God harder than ever before and anybody God send to me, I was going to witness to them even harder. So I girded up and went back in the house a new man, and wasn't feeling sorry for myself anymore. Weeks went by, and now it was time for me to go to court for the accident with the two little girls. I remind you that I was written a ticket of fifty dollars from the highway patrolman, in which was a blessing because it surely could have been more. So when I got to court, I knew I didn't have the fifty dollars to pay so I planned in my mind to asked if I could pay later along with any other charges I may have. Outside the courtroom were crowded, where people were there to handle their cases, also. I saw the highway patrolman who had my case across the room, so I pressed my way toward him. I got his attention and asked him could I pay later because I didn't have the money right then. He said I remember you, then he said, don't worry about it and tore up the ticket and said forget about it, you don't even have to be here. I didn't here from this anymore and I praised the Lord even harder than before.

I total loss my car God blessed me with and at first I was feeling down because I was thinking the car was not worth enough money to get another car. But when the insurance settlement was done, they paid my car off, plus gave me a check for seven hundred dollars. I praised the Lord and told everybody I could think of about the favor of God. So as I was looking for another car, I wanted a truck but they were all too high, so I seen a van to improvise for the truck. Because my friend Walt was there and he told me maybe God has other plans for you with the van. He didn't know that he was prophesying a thing we couldn't see, you'll see in a later chapter in the book.

During this time I had already told my girlfriend about her standards and morals and how God gives us freedom. Not knowing, I was about to be tested. My daughter needed me to take her to Atlanta to see her mother's family. Finally, I was able to come back to see them after ten years. Now, I was a changed man from whom they knew before. I was thinking maybe they had changed also, but after being around my brother-in-law, I found out they hadn't changed at all. I was trying to fit in and not go to far, and thank God it worked. After leaving them, I went across town to see my nephew-in-law. He was just like I used to be when I was at the top of my game. I settled in with him before I got back on the road toward home. Before I knew it, I was hitting all the hot spots with him. I knew he sensed the change in me by the way I was talking but regardless of that he didn't want to see the change. I was already in a compromising state of mind, so I went along with almost everything that was going on, but knowing I wouldn't go as far as I would before, because of what and Whom I knew now. We went to a jumping nightclub and I found myself partying hard, dancing down low with the girls, drinking and reminiscing on old times. I spent my last money out that night partying, which I had for traveling back home. The next day it was time for me to go, I asked my nephew-in-law to give me some money to get back home. He then began to go to work on my mind. He had spoke to me once before about getting back into the game but I opposed it because of Whom I was living for now. I guess this was his perfect time to catch me by surprise and he did. He told me I wouldn't have to suffer, being broke all the time. He then tossed me three pounds of marijuana on the table and said, there's more where those came from. Then he said, if you can get something started up in Greenville, you can get as many as you want. That quick, my mind was in a fixed state. I told him to let me think about it, and he gave me the money to get back home.

I got on the highway and my mind was really messed up, I didn't even realize it, but I was thinking very seriously on how I was going to pull this off. Satan was feeding my mind with crazy thoughts, telling me, look at your situation, you're broke and God have been feeding your mind about a business. Satan told me, that was far fetched from me. Satan actually told me that God was pumping my head up with a dream that was impossible without money. Then he reminded me of how I used to have it in his world. He told me, you know how to kick it up, otherwords, make money, then you can get your business open right away. As I was listening to this, my mind was really trying to figure this thing out. I was thinking how could I do this thing without my family knowing about it. Right at this moment, I had pushed the Holy Spirit aside. I wasn't thinking about God seeing me. I thought all I had to do was get the product and issue it out amongst my nephew and other young guys already involved in dirty business. All the way up the road, I was in deep concentration on how I was going to pull this thing off and still stay in church. I even thought if I could do it just for a little while, until I got enough money to open up a business and then I could get back Holy.

I finally got home and this thing was heavily on my mind. The first person I called was my friend Mike, who I knew could identify with me. I was thinking for sure he would go along with me and help me come up with a plan. I told him about the deal and he retaliated, telling me that my nephew-in-law knew what buttons to push with me. Then he went on to say that he was against it because he had been watching me and how God had been showing up in my life. He told me also, that he couldn't understand how his grandma and older people of the church were blessed with so much stuff, without a lot of money. He said, one thing he have come to know was that God can bless you without money. Right then, my soul and spirit were taken to a new light. It was like an angel had spoken through Mike to remind me of what I had experienced with the Lord since I've been on this side. The first thing I was reminded of was the accident I just had and how God blessed me in a mighty way with no charge against me nor my license. And how God provided right away a more updated vehicle for me with no money out my pocket. How could I forget so soon, the amazing favors God had done in my life. I couldn't believe I fell so deeply for satan's lie and how I was turned toward him so quickly. This is why, I love God's keeping power because when we can't keep ourselves, God steps in and sustains us, thank you Jesus.

After my conversation with Mike, I rebuked the devil and his demons in the name of Jesus. I told Satan he's a liar and the truth wasn't in him. By this incident I was made stronger by knowing how tricky satan is. The Holy Spirit reminded me when I told the church, I refused to let satan steal my joy, he tried by wrecking my car and to be honest with you my joy was gone for a minute and I cried like a baby. Then I realized through the Holy Spirit what was going on so I told satan it was a personal thing now. Guess what, he took it personal with the Atlanta trip and if it hadn't been for the Lord on my side, I would've made a big mistake. When He said in His Word, My sheep knows My voice, my spirit instantly heard Him through my friend Mike. If my spirit wouldn't have been submissive to the Holy Spirit, I would've missed it. Even though my flesh was stirred up, my spirit were submissive. Satan knew my weaknesses before I met the Holy Spirit so he tried to use my past desires I had in the world to lure me back to the world. And the bad thing about it was, I almost fell for it. That's why, I thank God for His Grace and Mercy because when we can't keep ourselves out of harm's way, He will keep us. This was another victory and I cried at His feet for not allowing me to fall.

But afterwards, I was still in the state of mind of compromising with the world. Proving to myself and my girlfriend that the liberty Apostle Paul was speaking about was the liberty or freedom to do almost anything I wanted as long as I stayed in the guide lines. The same guy God used to save me from making a serious mistake was now being used by satan to draw me in the web he had set for me. Mike called me and told me he had a surprise for me. He never told me the surprise or where we were going until we arrived at the place. I was already in a wild state of mind, awaiting to go out of town with my wife and kids, later in the same night. I was moving fast in this freedom I had, thinking I was alright socializing and compromising with my friends. Mike and I went into this nightclub and we sat down and I drunk a beer or two with him, then Mike told me I was in for a big surprise. Now Mike knew I was living a christian life but he felt me compromising and put me to the test. So while sitting drinking our beer, here comes some women dancers coming out to dance. Mike said watch this, these girls are going to get wild. And as I watched, I looked like I hadn't looked before, I couldn't believe my eyes, these girls started taking off all their clothes. I knew deep down in my soul that I was in the wrong place and needed to get out of there right away. But the more I watched the more my flesh was building up. The conviction of the Holy Spirit was in my mind but my flesh exited it out. I was in satan's territory and I myself was no match for him. I was helpless and subdued by temptation and lust. I got wild in that place and Mike was making things worst by paying the girls to rouse me up even more. It was like satan had set me up for this one. When we came out of there I instantly felt ashamed of what I've done in God's sight. I was very ashamed and convicted.

But regardless, I left them and went straight to my wife's house to prepare for the trip. I jumped from one scene into another without pausing, it was like I was on a roller coaster. See, my family and I were trying to reunite again, from being separated for twenty years, hoping we could pick up the pieces. We drove one hundred and fifty miles to get on a plane to fly three thousand miles to California. I was led to do this because my girlfriend had put it in my mind to try to reconcile my marriage back as the Bible says in 2 Corinthians 7. Since my girlfriend and I had gone our separate ways to see what God had for us, I figured this was the perfect time for me to reconcile. We finally arrived in California, where my wife and I hadn't been for twenty years. I was very excited about the trip, getting to see everybody again and this time along with two of my daughters and their best friend. I wasn't completely loose or at myself because my mind was still on my girlfriend or should I say ex-girlfriend, so I thought. But anyway, I thought to myself, I might as well shake it off and try to reunite with my family.

We first went over her aunt's house, which was where everybody met. We ate merry and had a fun time. Then we got put up in a Hotel and my daughters and their friend were in one room and my wife and I were in another room together. We went to bed together and got intimate with each other because of lust. It just seemed so different after twenty years. I felt a coldness from her and I'm sure she felt a coldness from me also. But I said to myself, this is it, I need to know if I can make it with my family again. I was really enjoying my daughters because I had never spent time with them like this before. We went to Malls, downtown L.A. and all over the place.

We were really there to celebrate my wife's cousin 50th birthday. The weekend had arrived and it was time to celebrate. She ordered about thirteen

Limousines to take us to the Yacht that she had rented for a few hours. It was very amazing to me and almost reminded me of the old days, so I was trying to hold my composure because I knew I was a changed man. As we were riding in the Limos, everybody were pulling out something to drink except my wife and I. She was really holding her composure in drinking, all this time I didn't know she had quit drinking. We all entered the boat and settled in, then the boat took us on a small tour. The party had started with music, drinks and dancing. I couldn't believe my eyes, I was in the middle of a scene like this, chillin without a worry in the world, it was like a dream come true. What do I do in a scene like this? except follow the crowd. Before I knew it I was at the bar ordering a drink. One drink after another and one dance after another, I was having a good time, I thought, not knowing I was being watched by my own family. I was swinging pretty good on and off the floor. One of my daughters shouted out, "daddy I'm gonna have to tell the Pastor about you laying your hair down". I told her yeah, I'm having a good time and this is my time. We celebrated on that boat for a while, then we left there and went to the hotel room to change attires without wasting any time.

    My wife's cousin was also giving a banquet at one of the ballrooms. So we all changed into something real formal and met in the ballroom to be seated. All of my family sat together at the same table. Everybody were drinking on something except for my wife. A comedian clown came out to entertain us. I was feeling real nice at this time and was about to forget who I was. I took off my suit jacket and pulled my shirt out like I used to do it in the old days. Now that I think about it, I was looking like an immature fool. I knew without a shout of a doubt, if God hadn't changed me, I would have been a bigger fool than I ever been. As the old saying goes, "ain't nothing like an old fool"! But anyway, we continued watching the comedian and enjoying the jokes. Instead of cheering and applauding, I was saying, Amen and applauding. My daughter reminded me twice, "daddy quick saying Amen, You're not in church". Then I had to come to myself and watch what I was doing. I still continued applauding and having a good time with my family. Then all of a sudden, my daughter who had been warning me all night about church made me very angry about the way she was treating her mother. I got on her case right there at the table. Her mother and sister were trying to cool me down, so I left it alone and got back into watching the show. Finally it was over, we went back to our rooms, the girls in their room and my wife and I in ours.

    I think I had a little too much to drink because it was making an effect on me. My mind kept reminding me how my daughter acted. So I jumped up, went to their room and started blasting her out again. This time a little worst because in my mind I thought she was being selfish and treating her mother very badly. I gave her a piece of my mind and told her that her sister and mother were afraid of telling her the truth about herself. Then she got upset and started screaming back at me, then her mother and sister started in on me and raked me out. Now I was in the room by myself with everybody mad at me. That was the longest night of my life, here I was with my girls twenty years later trying to discipline them, it was something else wrong with this picture besides too much to drink.

The next day we slept in the house with their kinfolk. My wife and I slept in the same room and the same bed with the coldest attitudes between the two of us. I truly believed that we had our mind on someone else, we didn't touch or speak to each other at all. As our time drew near, the next morning we got up rushing to get ready to go to the airport. Everybody concentrating on their luggage and accessories with a silence as if everybody had their mind on the night before. I felt so bad after knowing how terrible I acted toward my family. Without a shout of a doubt, I knew it was the alcohol that caused me to blurt out so uncontrollable. Even though, what I was saying and meaning was the truth, I still came out with it the wrong way. As we were flying home, my mind was telling me, I was an outsider with them now. They were all married to each other and I'll just be in the way with my new way of living. Our plane landed in Atlanta and we left there and drove one hundred and fifty miles toward home. At this time my wife and I discussed everything and she agreed with me about her and the kids were married to each other and that I'd been gone too long. So we were practically saying, it was not going to work with us coming back together as a family. We got home and emptied the car and said goodbye to each other. We all were in a daze, because we thought we were going on a reunited vacation to get back together. But instead, it seemed like a departure.

The next day I had a reconciling mind, I said to myself maybe I'm giving up too quick and wasn't giving it a chance. I called her and told her I was coming down, when I got there my mind was on trying to get my family back. I played and played with my grandsons while my wife was cooking. I just knew we were enjoying each other until there was a knock at the door and my wife went to the door and by my surprise, I looked and there stood her old boyfriend coming to see her. Then my daughters came in and it was like a family affair, except for one addition. I thought maybe she would get rid of him but instead she invited him to dinner. On top of that she made me fix my own plate in which she normally do. So all of us finished dinner and I went back to playing with my grandsons, waiting on her to get rid of him. The next thing I knew they were playing cards, laughing and having fun together. I was speechless and disappointed because I thought it was so disrespectful. Right at this moment, I had a flashback from the past and decided I didn't want to have a part of this anymore. My conversation with God was, "I tried but I guess it's over". I innocently made myself toward the door, saying goodbye to everyone, while looking in the eyes of my daughters as if they finally seen the truth, that I wasn't all the bad guy. I kissed my wife on the cheek right in front of him as a farewell kiss.

Right away, my mind was focused on my girlfriend, I thought to myself, I knew without a shout of a doubt that we were supposed to be together. I thought of all the morals and standards she was telling me to live by, was right. God had showed me and opened my eyes to the truth. He let me know I couldn't hang out with my friends that were going in bad places. And that I couldn't drink alcohol and party like everybody else. My soul was convicted and the Spirit grieved. I went right home and called my girlfriend and told her I loved her and I didn't want to ever let her go. Then I called my friend and told him we couldn't hang out anymore and we were about to become enemies. Because he was still selling drugs while I was testifying against it. I told him the two don't mix, he got upset about it at first, then he finally accepted it. Then the young lady on my job, who I wrongly told she can party as long as she didn't get wild. I had to apologize to her about making that statement and asked her for forgiveness. I told her I was wrong about telling her that, because when you put yourself in these places, then you are in satan's territory for him to throw all kinds of temptation at you. If you are not being led to these places by the Holy Spirit, then you are open game for satan. So I made my amends to everyone I had misinformed about morals and standards. And most of all I repented and asked God for forgiveness and got back into the right standards with God.

THE MARTIN LUTHER
KING EXPERIENCE

While sitting here on my mother's screened in porch enjoying the cool air from the evening summer breeze, I started meditating on the Lord's word. But as I was meditating I couldn't help for thinking about my financial situation. My mind kept carrying me back to when I was married and had a good job and everything I touched seemly turned to gold. I was just wondering what happened, why is it that everything I touch now turns to rags. It's like everything dissolves to nothing. The highest amount I get to is maybe five hundred dollars and then back to nothing. Even now, since I've found the Lord I ask Him, what is going on? Why can't I move like I once had? So while meditating on the Lord's word, the Holy Spirit took me to the book of Corinthians. I read the book of second Corinthians from chapter 1 to chapter 13, but chapter twelve really caught my attention when I read how Apostle Paul spoke about a thorn in his flesh. And his situation was kind of making me feel like I had a thorn in my flesh.

Prior to this thought, I had just recently been checking out tapes and doing some research on Dr. Martin Luther king. I listened to all his speeches and viewed his marches and understood the work he did in the Lord. God was enhancing my spirit with a vision He showed me a long time ago and slowly but surely I was grasping on to it. He was assuring me that it was going to be a long and prestigious process and if I endured and stayed in obedience to His Word, I will see His Glory and Salvation come into play. Now in an earlier chapter satan tried to convince me the vision God showed me was impossible, he also tried to induce me to go backwards to bring the vision to light. And I have to say, he almost had me. While I was doing this research with Dr. Martin Luther king I ran across a scripture that really put me in prospective to where I was going. It was in the book of Genesis, chapter 37:19,20. Here Joseph brothers conspired to kill him because of the dream he told them. They said to one another, look, "this dreamer is coming"! Come therefore, let us now kill him and cast him into some pit, and we shall say, some wild beast has devoured him! we shall see what comes of his dreams. Immediately, I thought about this scripture and how satan comes quickly to try to take away your dreams and all your hope.

Now I see why Apostle Paul had a thorn in his flesh because God's power and grace shows up through our weaknesses. And with our weaknesses God still puts a dream or vision in us to give us hope. And right here with this scripture, when everything seemed hopeless, God's grace manifested itself in me to make me stay in the race. It kind of reminded me of the greyhound dog race with the rabbit placed in front of the dog in order to get him to run the race. He didn't know if he was ever going to catch that rabbit but he ran his heart out trying. I believed God had placed this dream in me to chase and the only way to catch this dream was to be obedient to His word and fine tuned to His voice to be able to hear what direction to take. It was like the time I had in jail, when God put in my spirit the choice of getting what He had to give and teach me or staying in jail longer until I got it. But I chose to get what He had to give me and teach me, so I could get out on parole. I got out on parole and got even more of a gift, the best gift a man could ask for and that was a relationship with God, Jesus and the Holy Spirit.

Weeks went by, while I was in deep meditation with studying God's word and listening to tapes and cassettes of certain preachers, bishops and prophetesses and plus reading the Word of God. I was getting rooted deeper and deeper in the Word any kind of way I could get it, I was hungry and thirsty for it. Some of my friends, family and even my mother asked me, do you think you are getting too much, being in your room sun up to sun down. I even wondered myself, was I getting in too deep? Nevertheless, I was hungry and God was making sure I got full. At this time I didn't know God was preparing me for a time to come.

I stayed closed in for a while until God started planting confidence in my spirit. I was beginning to set my eyes on a shrimping business. I was very curious about getting started with it. Then one Sunday while sitting in church, the Pastor preached a sermon titled, "don't be afraid of the deep". He preached out of Luke 5:4, when Jesus told Simon, known as Peter, "launch out into the deep and let down your net for a catch". This word to me was confirmation from the Holy Spirit. And on this word, I was ready to make a move toward what I'd been anticipating on. I had already been talking to this Mexican, whose name was Carlos and who had been in the fish and shrimp business before. So I asked him was he ready to make a trip down Charleston and he was more ready than I. We traveled three hundred miles on this trip in his small beat up pick-up truck with no spare, in which I didn't know until we got on the road. We rode around in the town with two big coolers on board and not having a clue where to look. We rode all around Charleston and found nothing so we had to spend the night in a hotel room together. This was an experience of my life being linked with a person with totally different customs and I didn't know him outside of work. But we did have a chance to talk about some key issues concerning life and life with Jesus. He tested me with different religions and beliefs and hard-core questions about life. And each time, I would witness to him about the love of Christ that was in me, he would say, he love God too. So I mentioned the kind of love where you don't want to sin because you don't want to hurt God or yourself.

Anyhow, the next day we got up and went on the search again. Finally, God blessed us with a place with plenty shrimp at a good price. We got about one hundred pounds of shrimp and came back to Greenville to sell. The next day we put up a sign and sat all day on a corner and nothing sold. The next day we decided to go to the neighborhoods, black and white people and still nothing. Then Carlos suggested that we go to the Mexican neighborhoods. I think this was the best suggestion he could have made because we sold out like it was going out of style. From then on we made regular trips and sold out each time. He was getting popular in the Mexican neighborhoods, which made him drank more and fooling with prostitutes more. Then he started adding other people in on the business. They were feeding him with poisonous information. He was beginning to get desperate and started selling bad shrimp. I told him I couldn't do this anymore, so we separated the shrimp and he was letting me keep the money so he wouldn't spend it up on the girls. Then he started listening to folks, telling him I was cheating him so he came back after his money. It was no problem with me, I honored everything he wanted. Then I stopped for a while and he kept going on the trips with his friends to get shrimp. One day, he came over my house burdened down and wanted to cry. He explained his situations and problems and told me he was sorry. I accepted his apology and told him about the life he was living. I then explained to him the reason I told him about the difference of the love of Christ we had. I broke it down to his level by mentioning his wife and how he sees other girls behind her back. I said, "if you really loved her, you wouldn't do this wrong to her". This is almost the same thing people do to Jesus. We say we love Him but don't regard His feelings when we do wrong on purpose. Carlos listened to me and agreed to go to bible studies with me and God was really touching him in these classes. We finally split up and as of today we are still friends. I believed deep in my heart he would really loved to come close to God. But it was just a matter of time, praise the Lord, some day he will.

God has a funny way of doing some things in our lives. He'll work on something now that will not manifest until a year or years later. The mini van I got from the Lord after the wreck, gave me a way to go and get my own shrimp. My friend Walt had already prophesied about the van doing something else besides carrying shrimp. He said, God was getting ready to bless you even more with this van and maybe that's why He's not allowing you to get a truck because He's getting you ready for a building. See I wanted the truck to be able to go to neighborhoods to sell the shrimp. But I pondered on what he had prophesied and didn't make anymore trips. Instead, my mind was being changed to get a building. Even though, I didn't have any money I still contemplated on getting a business. I mentioned to the Pastor one day about the sermon he preached, titled "don't be afraid of the deep". Then I told him I was interested in a business that I've been doing on the side. He followed up by telling me, he was interested in opening a business also and maybe we could come together. He said, he would front all the money if I find a place. Right away, I was very excited about him volunteering to come in with me to start this business. I wanted to open a fresh fish market on one side and a seafood restaurant on the other.

I searched all over town for the right building and right location. I didn't have a clue on how to run either one but I was trusting the Lord to guide me and give me wisdom. Every week for three months, I searched and searched and couldn't find anything. The Pastor would ask me have I found anything yet. He even came to my house and affirmed me of his certainty of the loan he would provide. When he left I was so excited and was thanking the Lord for His favor. I finally found a building, in which I thought would make a good place, even though it needed renovation inside and out. I had became very desperate and anxious about this proposition, I was going on my own instincts. Really my anxiety would make me jump on the first thing I saw and thought would work, I was full of optimism. I was excited and was thinking anything would work with the amount of money the Pastor was talking about.

Time went by and I was still anticipating on what the Pastor had offered but to my knowledge the Pastor started ignoring me more and more. I tried to remind him of what he said, but he pushed me to the side. He was getting into situations concerning Dr. Martin Luther King's birthday and he was leading the crowd. So I continued studying the Word in deep meditation. And as I was studying and doing what I do in church, I couldn't help for noticing and watching the move on Dr. Martin Luther King's birthday. Just about all the Pastors in town were putting pressure on the county councilmen to observe his birthday like every other town. Seemed like the more the Pastors were pressuring, the more the county councilmen were rejecting them. I believed, everybody in town were getting involved. There were crowds flooding the courtroom and the outside. People all over were getting into uproars over Dr. Martin Luther King's birthday, there were marches, standouts and boycotts.

Our church Sunday school classes were teaching and talking down on people of the county council with prejudice stirring up in themselves. Now it was time for me to step in and speak the truth. Every time one of the teachers spoke rudely about the other races, I told them, if you all talk about them, what make you any better? Each one looked at me strangely as if they were saying, "he's a new comer and he just don't understand what's going on". But the matter got worst and the Pastor was preaching about it every Sunday boosting the people on. I started to understand why I wasn't getting any response on the ordeal we spoke on, concerning the business. He was focusing on his own agenda and pushing mine aside, the more I thought about it the more angrier I got. I took myself off the front pews and went back to the mid section pews. I had became very bitter about the ordeal he promised me and the idea of him talking like a man of hatred in the pulpit. My mind had really gotten frustrated with all the Pastors, even the ones on Television at this moment. Because they would preach prosperity to people and didn't try to help them financially. I was feeling a lot of remorse because the preachers made their money preaching and I thought to myself, everybody were not made for preaching. So show me how to start a business without any money. After these thoughts running wild through my mind came to a halt, I figured I was just acting out of pity for myself.

And to keep myself from swerving to the right or the left, I made myself get back into meditation with God's Word. As I was in deep meditation, the Holy Spirit revealed to me clearly a scripture in the Bible concerning the ordeal the Pastor had made with me. The Holy Spirit had reminded me of the sermon the Pastor had preached a few weeks ago. It was concerning this same scripture, which was Joshua 5:13-15. This scripture read; And it came to pass, when Joshua was by Jericho, he lifted up his eyes and looked and behold, a Man stood opposite of him with a sword drawn in His hand. Joshua went to Him and asked, are You for us or for our adversaries? He said, neither, but as Commander of the army of the Lord, I have come. And Joshua fell on his face to the earth and worshipped, and said to Him, what does my

Lord say to His servant? Then the Commander of the Lord's army said to Joshua, take off your sandals, for the place where you stand are Holy. And what the Holy Spirit was speaking into my spirit was behold, for I am with you, sending a man of God to your house was confirmation and assurance to let you know I hear you. Then the Holy Spirit told me, there would be nobody able to take the glory for what God is about to do in your life. So I rejoiced in the Lord and was delighted to be in His presence. I had a new mind set and a new spirit. And I knew I had to get back on track and stay focus on His purpose for my life. I studied night and day on His Word to show myself approved in any circumstance and to be more effective when I witness to an unbeliever. I was no longer angry at the Pastor for leading me on because God had revealed His revelation to me.

But as I continued going to church the Pastor and his crew were still debating on the issues of Martin Luther king's birthday and with the white councilmen that were seated on the council board. On this particular Bible study night, I had just come out from under the presence of God and was filled with the Holy Spirit. As I was anticipating on some good Bible studying, I walked in on the Pastor still discussing matters from the council meetings. He then started talking about the President and how he was lying about mass destruction over in the Middle East. The Pastor also said, the President took advantage of Sadam Hussein, just for the oil. He might be right but the Holy Spirit had already revealed something to me concerning this situation a week ago. The Holy Spirit had pointed out to me that there have never been a Presidential miscount in US history. Therefore in this case they miscounted twice and it seemed like Gore was cheated out the race. But I believed with all my heart, God knew Vice President Gore couldn't perform the task God wanted done as effective as President Bush. So I repeated this same statement to the Pastor and some of his colleagues. Then I went a little further to back up what I was saying, by taking them to a scripture concerning a similar matter, which was in Deuteronomy chapter 9:1 thru 6. Moses was telling Israel, they were getting ready to possess the land of some mighty folks, more powerful than them. In verses 4 thru 6 Moses said, do not think in your heart, after the Lord your God has cast them out before you, saying, because of my righteousness, the Lord has brought me in to possess this land; but it is because of the wickedness of these nations that the Lord is driving them out from before you. It is not because of your righteousness or the uprightness of your heart that you go in to possess their land, but because of the wickedness of these nations that the Lord your God drives them out before you and that He may fulfill the Word which the Lord swore to Abraham, Isaac and Jacob.

Therefore understand that the Lord your God is not giving you this good land to possess because of your righteousness, for you are a stiff-neck people.

Then I told the Pastor and his colleagues, God wasn't interested in the oil or the mass destruction or the vendetta people talk about from George Bush Sr. encounter with Hussein. I explained, what God didn't like was the fact that Hussein was building images of himself and acting as if he was God in front of the people. And on top of this, he was killing innocent people. So God's wrath fell on Hussein and the people who followed him. I could tell the Pastor was getting angry because he was talking over my conversation to drown me out. Nevertheless, I spoke what was in my heart and was very much sincere about it. The Pastor went on to say to his colleagues in a round about way, "I was a rookie or a newcomer to the Word and I needed more time to learn". After saying my part, I immediately got quiet, hoping I didn't offend anybody. The Pastor was probably right about me being a newcomer or a rookie at this because I had fire shut up in my bones and I had to get it out. Even twenty years from now I hope I still have this fire, zeal and burning desire inside of me. Sometimes as time passes by, I think Christians get relaxed in their comfort zones. And they tend to get passive or unconcerned about the Truth and the Word.

The Holy Spirit had revealed to me in John 4:22-24, which stated, you worship what you do not know, we know what we worship, for Salvation is of the Jews. But the hour is coming and now is, when the true worshippers will worship the Father in Spirit and Truth. For the Father is seeking such to worship Him. God is Spirit, and those who worship Him must worship in spirit and truth. I told the Pastor and his colleagues, when I heard this scripture, it kind of stunned me. Because I thought when you worship in spirit you are worshipping in truth. But when Jesus said spirit and truth, I had to dig a little deeper by asking the Holy Spirit what does this mean, spirit and truth. The "and" separated the two. Then I told them, the Holy Spirit revealed to me that when you worship in spirit, you can be in the Spirit one minute and ready to curse someone out the next minute. Otherwords, people can jump in and out of the Spirit. But when they're really in the Truth, which is Jesus Christ, they'll be living a lifestyle like Jesus of Nazareth. Therefore, they won't praise God with one breath and curse man with another. After these words, I calmed down and was silent because I didn't want to cause any trouble. I even asked God not to act harshly toward me for being upfront to His anointed.

I told my girlfriend about it and she said, she would never speak to her Pastor like that. I felt badly, when she told me this, so I tried to explain to her that I was only speaking the truth. After this, I really prayed to God about this situation because I didn't want to cross the line in speaking the truth to my Pastor. Then the Holy Spirit showed me a scripture in Matthews. I was feeling what King David was feeling when he was going up against God's anointed. So I followed the Holy Spirit to Matthews 10:24,25 and from there I went to Luke 6:40, which gave me a better understanding. It stated, "A disciple is not above his teacher, but everyone who is perfectly trained will be like his teacher". This scripture made me feel more better because after reading this, it was like the Holy Spirit was confirming to me that I was just learning more and speaking what I've learned. I told my girlfriend about the scripture and she said again she wouldn't dare approach her Pastor like that. I told her I didn't do it out of rage but out of love. When Sunday rolled back around the Pastor was in a whole different state of mind. He was back to himself again, full of the Holy Spirit. I had to run up to hug him and tell him how much I loved him when he let God use him because that's what it's about in all of us. Our flesh is a mess and we must allow the Holy Spirit to come in to dwell and operate in us to make us a better person. My Pastor stepped down from that rally and got back to work for the Lord.

The rallies were still carrying on with other Pastors, politicians and county councilmen. They were in out rage with each other, coming to the point of fighting each other through hatred. I took it upon myself to write each one of the councilmen by E-mail. I wrote these words; I Robert Harris a concern citizen, think men and women, preachers and county councilmen should come together and see things through God's eyes and not their own personal feelings. Martin Luther King was a great man of God's own heart. He set out on a mission for God to bring people together, to refuse him or look at him ordinary is to refuse God or look at Him ordinary. God should be noticed more, recognized and respected more for what He does on earth through men. God want people to come together not for their statue but for their hearts. 1 Samuel 16:7 says, for the Lord seeth not as man seeth, for man looketh on the outward appearance but God looketh on the heart. So let's come together and compromise peacefully through God's eyes. Martin Luther King followed God every step of the way in this dream he had. No matter what kind of adversity he came up against, he kept his mind stayed on Jesus and followed God's plan. By this, my eyes were opened, and I knew if I wanted anything to work in my life, I had to do it in God's will and not my own. I've already tried it for forty years my way and it didn't work.

And as Apostle Paul says about this thorn in his flesh; God spoke to him saying, My grace is sufficient for you, for My strength is made perfect in weakness. Then Apostle Paul said, therefore most gladly I will rather boast in my infirmities, that the power of Christ may rest upon me. Then he said, therefore I take pleasure in infirmities, in reproaches, in needs, in persecutions, in distress, for Christ sakes. For when I am weak, then I am strong. I know I can't compare with Apostle Paul and I wouldn't dare try. This process God is sending me through is for my benefit, in that I grow stronger in Him. So when I'm at my weakest point, then I am at my strongest in Christ.

THE DRAMA AT NTM

After a five month journey from one job to another by following a former employee in my own will, instead of checking with the Holy Spirit to see if it was alright with God to make this move. I quit NTM to make more money and believe me I paid for this mistake. But regardless, on this journey I learned some things from God and was able to witness to some people in spite of my mistake. I had heard the employee that I followed had went back to NTM, a plastic recycling Plant and he was now a Supervisor. So I called him about getting my job back. He told me to wait and see what he can do, because they were making it hard for people returning for their old jobs. I had a deep feeling that this was an opportunity for me to get back in there. Two weeks went by and he finally called and told me to come in, I thanked God every step of the way. They hired me back on a new shift around new people. When I came in, I got acquainted with everyone but I still did what I've always done on the previous shift I was on and that was staying in my own setting. Quite often while on break I would go some where secluded and study much as I could. I loved being in the presence of the Lord. I thought that was all it was to do, staying in the presence of the Lord.

But then, this certain woman came to me and told me I needed to change my format. She went on to tell me why, "because everybody stays together on this shift", simple fact was because a guy got killed on their shift doing a job by himself. Plus, she said it wasn't good for me to separate myself like this. So every once in a while, I would come into the canteen where everyone would be jive talking to one another. And it seemed like the more I went in, the more I wanted to go in. I would jive talk a little too but not beyond standards. But I did get into compromising and relaxing beyond measure. Otherwords, I would bypass the profanity they were talking and it seemed like they knew I had dropped my guards. Because at times they would get worst and include me in on some of their schemes. Everybody were kind of like family with their own little secrets on each other.

My friend and now Supervisor, who helped me get back in there were becoming more closer friends. We were hanging out cooking different foods together, mainly fish. We started contemplating on frying fish on the street corners to sell. We built our courage up and got our equipment together and made our move. We did good on our first day out so we decided to go out a couple more times. Some days were good and some not so good. A friend of my Supervisor let us stand in front of his nightclub during the day every other Saturday. On the Saturday we weren't there they done it themselves, causing customers to question us about our prices and product. So I told my Supervisor let's get our own building so we can do our own thing. I searched in that area day in and day out for a building. I was very determined to get something in that area, I was beginning to think that the Holy Spirit wanted me in that area. Finally, I found a little building about a block from where we were. I checked into it and was able to get a look on the inside. It was stripped naked with cement floors, brick walls and no ceiling. Here I was again in an optimistic state of mind, excited about the building. I didn't have no equipment, no skills and most of all no money, but again I was determined. I convinced myself, I could cook outside until I made enough money to fix the place up like a restaurant. I went back and told my Supervisor I found a place right down the street from where we were for only four hundred dollars a month. Time went by and as we continued working, we had discussions on the building and he mentioned how much work we had to put in it, then he wanted me to look at this building down in his hometown already set up for a restaurant. So I said to myself why not because I was destined to open this fish camp so the easier the better. I found out later that I was an overly optimistic guy, I'll use my last breath trying to make a mountain out of an ant hill, and I don't know if that's good or bad. My Supervisor pointed me out to a couple of places but one in particular was strongly on my mind. But we kept working and just talking until our minds were on other things.

Then as I got back to studying the Word strongly, the Holy Spirit started revealing some things to me about my Supervisor. He was the baby boy of five siblings and they all gave him whatever he wanted. And he always wanted to compete with someone in everything he did. Everything he said and did was right and there was no other way. I was in full agreement with him at first, until the Holy Spirit started revealing to me these things about him, then I stopped being in full agreement with him. As I was saying no to him or refusing to go along with some of his pranks, he was beginning to get angry. Even in business with him God brightened my senses. The Holy Spirit took me even deeper with him by telling him satan was desiring to take his life and God was desiring him to be Saved. I touched him with some personal matters of his, to let him know I wasn't lying on the Holy

Spirit. I tried and tried to get him to get Saved but as normal he said, he wasn't ready.

The fish idea came to a standstill and we all went back to doing what we done best, worked. I studied much as I could whenever they weren't trying to add me to the group. The group of employees that worked with me were very relaxed and had their way with the Supervisor. And just because I didn't get into the same relaxed scene, they were having a little animosity with me. I tried working diligently as much as I could, God had already showed me favor by abling me to work in the Lab. In which the guys on the floor would get jealous everytime I had to go in there. There were two of us on the floor as material handlers and a third man, who was much older around retiree age, who was our team leader. There was a lady in the Lab, in which I took her place when she was out. There was another young lady who worked with us, who really had her way with the Supervisor. Then a new young lady came in and joined the team and she was a bigger mess than the rest of them, once she saw how everybody else were working. They ran over the Supervisor because he didn't know how to say no.

I tried to mine my own business but I couldn't any longer. I had to tell him some of the mistakes he was making with his employees. Then I told him the people were watching him in the front offices. I told him I was concerned about him since we were friends. He told me to quit worrying about his job and he knew what he was doing. He got worst and worst with his employees and his production. Then he told me he was just a good guy and a lot of people can't get with good people. I began explaining to him the difference between a good man with Christ and a good man without Christ. A man who tries to please everybody for his own benefit is different than a man who pleases God and does His will. Because God's way and understanding is different than our understanding. I told him that's hard for people to get with. I went on to tell my Supervisor, God's wisdom was different than man's wisdom. Our wisdom ables us to do certain skills, and along with God's wisdom, it supersedes your wisdom to do even more excellent skills. He gives a clearer understanding and vision. I told him, I was concerned for him as a friend and I had the highest respect for him as a Supervisor.

His people got worst instead of better. The owner of the place brought in another Plant Manager to put everything in alignment and he was very rough. I got along with him very well but everybody else hated him. Everybody dodged him everytime he came around. I continued studying the Word to feed my spirit because I felt a lot of heat stirring up in the place. I was staying mostly to myself again and it bothered them for some reason. They were getting more hostile everytime I would come around. I was under the anointing at this time, soaking in what the Holy Spirit was teaching me. At this time I was also listening to Bishop T.D Jakes, Joyce Meyers, Bishop Noel Jones and a local Bishop in the name of William L. Bonner. And Noel Jones struck my attention the most at this particular time. The Holy Spirit would give a message through all of them for a certain time. I thank God for being able to record these sermons because I couldn't afford them at the time. Anyway, Bishop Noel Jones came with a powerful message concerning satan's attacks in a run of a day and how we need to get up and pray early in the morning for protection. I took it lightly because I knew I kept in contact with the Lord. But low and behold, did I make a mistake this particular day or should I say week! Not knowing the Holy Spirit was speaking through Bishop Noel Jones for my life at this particular time.

This certain lady of whom, recently in an earlier chapter asked me did God mine her going out to the nightclubs. And at that time I was in a compromising state of mind, so I wrongly answered her by saying God didn't mine as long as you didn't get wild. Then God showed me face to face that I was wrong for telling her that. I had to apologize for that statement, then I told her, I had it all wrong because the Holy Spirit revealed it to me that you can't hang out partying and expect God to look over it. She accepted my apology. Now, assuming everything was alright between us, I saw her coming from outside into the canteen smiling after seeing her new boyfriend, so I thought. I was amazed, seeing her smiling for a change from being in so much anger day after day. I told her, I've noticed you've been smiling more now and that's a good thing. Then I told her, since the new guy been around you've been in a good mood. And what did I say that for? She jumped down my throat like I stole something. She told me to stay out of her business, then called me a punk-b'tch, among other curse words. It shocked me so much that I was speechless. Not only that, she carried on in the canteen with more illiterate literature or profanity. She kept calling me a punk-b and my flesh was climbing the more I heard it. But thank God for the Holy Spirit in me because He helped me hold my composure. That one certain word she used, when I was in the world I would get furious to no end. It seemed like satan knows what strings to pull. I still felt bad though, all day long and this went on for a few days. Everyday I came in to work I felt the pain, we wouldn't even speak to each other.

Then finally, the Holy Spirit spoke to me to apologize to her. At first it seemed strange, since I thought she was in fault. But the Holy Spirit was telling me to go to her and it was hard. I didn't hesitate anymore after the second warning from the Holy Spirit. I went full blast because I wanted to be obedient to the Holy Spirit. I went in her work area and told her I was sorry and I asked her to forgive me. She looked at me very surprised and said okay. And later that day she also came to me and apologized. After seeing this, I thanked God even the more.

But it wasn't over with yet, as I said earlier everybody seemed like they had it in for me. I guess, because I didn't go for their program and I would speak up for what was right. Anyway, this particular day, when we came in to work, there was work backed up to our necks. It was three of us on the floor, an old man about sixty and a guy about thirty-eight. The thirty-eight year old guy did little as possible everyday. We complained to the Supervisor, but since they had been knowing each other for a long time, the Supervisor didn't phase him. He still did what he wanted. The old man and I was working our behind off and all we needed were just a little more help. So I went to him to ask him if he could help us out a little. He looked at me, holding his coffee cup as usual and told me you ain't my Supervisor. Then he said, I can do what I want to do. Right then, I snapped and grabbed him in the chest and ram him into the pipes. I told him, you don't know who you are talking to, I'll hurt you up in here. Luckily, a mechanic was standing around to come between us. I was very angry at this time and feeling everybody were teaming up on me. I was beginning to get in rage and my flesh was climbing.

This young man who was new on the job rode up on the forklift and asked me what was wrong with me. He knew me when I was on the streets and knew I had made a change in Christ. I just started telling him out of rage that they didn't know me around here. I told him, you know me though, you know I don't play. You know how I used to carry those guns on me and how I'll pull the trigger. Then I started putting him in it too. I told him, y'all think that I'm soft because I carry that Book with me, but you better let them know that I ain't no punk, I can flip to old Earl anytime. He left on the forklift and in five minutes he was back telling me to calm down. He said, don't you know the enemy is after you. He said, I'm not a christian but I studied the Word in jail and I know a little. Then he told me, they are mad at you because you're doing something they're not doing and that's being in the Word. He said you're doing something they desire but don't know how to do. The devil is coming through them to get to you, to make you fall but stay strong, he said. Right then after he left, I went and got on my knees to pray to my Lord and I broke down in tears. I cried because I knew God had sent him back on that forklift. It was like an Angel was in this guy telling me all of this. I was on the verge of breaking down but God spoke to me and kept me. This is why I say as I had said in a previous chapter, when God said My sheep know My voice, I recognized it again through this guy.

It's amazing how God can use anybody or anything to get His message through for our lives. Some people think God's word have to come through a great religious figure only. But God told Elijah in 1 Kings 19:11,12, to go out and stand on the mountain before the Lord. And behold, the Lord passed by and a great strong wind tore into the mountain and broke the rocks in pieces before the Lord, but the Lord wasn't in the wind; and after the wind an earthquake, but the Lord wasn't in the earthquake, and after the earthquake a fire, but the Lord wasn't in the fire, after the fire a small still voice. God said in His Word, His sheep know His voice. So please don't miss it by looking or listening for something else.

After I prayed and got my self together, the Holy Spirit spoke to me again to go and apologize to this guy I had grabbed in the chest. I told him I was sorry for what I did to him, I just got carried away with myself. So I really got myself back into the Word, trying to see what was going on. Then I thought about what Bishop Noel Jones was preaching about. He said, when God get you up in the morning pray for protection and to let you know how to be prepared for the unexpected. I listened to his sermon over and over again until it was down in my spirit. What was happening on my job was exactly what Bishop Noel Jones was speaking about. Then I prayed like I never prayed before. Because now I knew satan was on my case and God allowed him to attack me this way to take me to another level in character. And even shortly after these incidents, I was in another scrabble with a young kid who had questioned me about some situation and I gave him a straight up answer of correction on his behalf. He blew out of proportion and ran to the Supervisor about the situation. The Supervisor had everybody so spoil that they were no good for him or anybody else.

Finally the Supervisor, my friend came to talk to me one on one about myself. We stood face to face conversating about the christian world and the regular world. He told me he don't know how I can sit up here and call myself a christain. Then he said, "you are a poor excuse for a christian and that's why I don't want to become a christian" and be a hypocrite. I simply told him, first of all you wouldn't understand what I would have to say to you in the spirit, because you are coming to me in the flesh. I had the Bible in my lap reading it already so I told him I can show him the scripture right here in the Bible. Then he attacked me again about being in the Word, I told him to calm down so we can talk like men. I went on to tell him, you shouldn't attack me concerning the Word because you're not just attacking me now but you are attacking God and His Word and that's a dangerous thing. I told him if you're coming to attack me, then attack me and not the Word. I told him, I can be old Earl anytime I want to because my flesh is present with me at all times. There's nothing holding me from being old Earl, except for the Holy Spirit, who helps me to walk in newness. So that mean, I don't want to be the old Earl anymore but I rather be the new Earl in Christ. But regardless of what I was saying, he had his mind made up to get his point across. He told me, not only are you a poor excuse for a christian but you are lesser to be a man. He said he would never respect me as being a man again. If it's up to him, I will never get a promotion with him being Supervisor. He wiped the sweat off his entire head from the heat and the contention and then left. This was two hours of conversation that was quite interesting, knowing now how he really felt about me. But God is a good God and I knew for sure, He take care of His. The young lady and man who I had apologized to earlier, went out to get lunch and called back with car trouble. They needed someone to come and get them and guess who came and asked me to borrow my vehicle, my Supervisor. This happened in the same day with all three at my mercy and God made sure I recognized it. I gave him my keys to go get them and they all came back thanking me for the favor because they were all breaking the rules, even the Supervisor. But I just smiled and went on my way.

Now not only did the blacks have it in for me but the whites also, who were in that area. They also looked at me funny and pretended that everything was cool, but they had a look on their faces like I was the enemy. I did speak the truth when it was time to speak it without sugar coating it. By doing this, I stepped on a lot of toes, even my own if necessary. Now I see why they say Jesus offended the most people in the Bible. I told someone that and they couldn't believe it. They said He was a loving God and He wouldn't offend no one. I read a couple of scriptures to her and told her tough love hurts, otherwords the truth hurts.

I couldn't understand why people would like to have what you have, but hate you for having it. One of the girls in the bunch was pregnant and worked in the Lab. She left on maternity leave and her friend who kept a lot of confusion stirred up, wanted to work in the Lab in her place. She tried but didn't have enough experience so that left me to go in there. The Supervisor wanted her to go in there because they hung out in there before the pregnant lady left. But anyway, thanks to the Lord because the Lab was the best place in the plant besides the offices. It was a chance for me to really study the Word in my spare time and stay in the presence of the Lord. It's hard to stay in the presence of the Lord on the job, when you have people working around you, who don't care about what they say or do. And the sad thing about it is, I used to be just like that, not considering anything. I broke some bad habits the crew had, even the Supervisor. They tried to continue to meet up in the Lab, hanging out together with their profanity and nasty talking, and right away I rebuked it to their faces. I told them, I was on my job and I didn't have to tolerate them invading my space with all that profanity and nasty talking. They thought I was the rudest person in the whole place, nevertheless, things got more quiet and I was able to meditate in peace.

On my breaks I would go out to my vehicle to listen to Bishop William L Bonner, my favorite from the local gospel radio station. As of this day, I still listen to Bishop William L Bonner because he's like a father in the spirit to me, even though I've never met him. I constantly fed myself with all kinds of Gospel, even this preacher who came on at 11:00 PM, preaching about damnation and the ends of the world. I tried to gain as much knowledge of the Word as possible and it sunk in. I thank God for filling me with so much of His Word. He said those who hunger and thirst after righteousness shall be fed. My soul was getting in so much peace, it was like I was in another world. I've been in this condition a number of times but not like the first time when I met the Holy Spirit and was under the Anointing of the Holy Spirit. Everybody that came in the Lab felt the power of the Holy Spirit. I know they did because they all would speak about something Holy, except for my Supervisor because he was in rebellion with what I was doing. He would bring his rap music with his Jam Box in there to distract me. Even then, I would still try to witness to him and request him to get Saved and right away he would disappear. It seemed like I was fighting a losing battle at times, but deep inside I knew the Lord working through me was causing some effect with my fellow workers.

Then there were two guys who came aboard in the Word and they immediately found out that I was in the Word. Each one of them would come into the Lab quoting scriptures to let me know what kind of knowledge they had in the Word. And I told them, "I am so glad there's some fellow worshipers in the house, it makes my soul rejoice to know there is someone else who love the Lord like I do". Even the young lady who I had apologized to, noticed the two guys. She said to me, "you are not by yourself now, God sent you some help", I burst out hallelujah. I continued to work in the Lab until the young lady came back off maternity leave but while I was in there I was able to witness to a lot of people just dropping by to keep cool. I began to notice one of the guys that was in the Word. He stayed worried about something and kept his head down toward the floor all the time. I asked was everything alright, because to me a full grown christian don't suppose to be in this state, unless there's a burden somewhere. He explained to me why he was worried, at lease some of it. I prayed about the situation and the Holy Spirit gave me a solution to the problem to tell him. After I told him he immediately responded. I gave him a tape to listen to so he could get back in love with Jesus. I could tell he had fallen short and needed a serious revival to the soul. After this I didn't talk with this brother to much more.

Now the other brother in the Word kept coming around with his Porta-Bible, pulling up scriptures, in which I enjoyed so much. Everytime someone came to me to talk about the Bible and go to scriptures I would get so excited. I really got an enjoyment out of talking about the Word. My spirit would rumble, tumble and jump when I found someone interested in God. So while looking at the brother in Christ scan through his Porta Bible, we discussed how good it was to be in God's kingdom. I could tell he had a lot of knowledge of the Bible. As days went by, I had a discernment flash through my mind. For a minute my mind would wonder if these guys were serious like me or were they just up for competition in the Word. Because for one, I never seen them witness to anyone and maybe for this reason they were old converts and I was new and excited. But nevertheless, I continued to study and witness.

God enabled me to see some glorious things these next few days. Both of the people I had disputable confrontations with came back to my view. One was the young lady who cursed me out. She came in the Lab one day and said she was scared and wanted protection. And to be honest with you, I was astonished and surprised to hear her talking like this. Because she was the tough rugged type, she was pretty as a Georgia peach but she was fast and rough as though she was raised in the hood. After she told me this, I had to think on what to do now. So right then, I tapped into the Holy Spirit to give me an answer. Then I asked her did she want to get Saved, I explained to her the procedure. And she said yes, so I told her to come back later because I had to pray about this to make sure it was okay to do so. I prayed for authority and the right to pronounce her into the kingdom through our Lord and Savior Jesus Christ. She came back in about an hour later and said she was ready. So I opened my Bible, but first I prayed with her and spoke to God about her heart and to let her know what I was about to do was coming straight from God. Which I already knew because Jesus said in His Word that no one cometh unto Him unless they are drawn from the Father (John 6:44). Then I read Romans 10:9-10 to her and held her hands and asked her did she understand and she said yes. I prayed the repentance prayer and she repeated after me. Afterwards, I told her you are Saved and have accepted Christ openly. When she left, I was the most happiest man in the world, simply because after all the things satan was putting in her mind about me, God turned it around for His divine purpose. I was shouting for joy with the Angels in heaven.

I told one of the brothers in Christ about the good news and he said a negative thing about her. And by this, I knew only three things and one was either he wasn't serious in the ministry or he had been in the ministry too long, where as he had lost interest. Thirdly he had a lot of maturing to do in the ministry, even though he was an old convert. But moreover, I was exceedingly glad and wished that more people would make this move toward God. Not only accepting Jesus for our Savior but allowing Him to deliver us from our past life and to really learn and know Him personally, so that we could have that passion of love for Him, like He has for us.

It was getting time for me to come out of the Lab and get back on the floor with two people who could have wished I would go away. Seem like God's perfect timing is always on time because I went into the Lab at the right time for perfect peace. One of the guys were the old white man about 60 years old who all the time talked about retiring. The other guy was the 38 year old black man who I had pushed in the chest for being a slacker and getting smart about it. But before I got on the floor good, there was a drug testing going on with everybody in the Plant. Three people were fired and one of them was the guy I pushed in the chest, the other one was a newcomer who had laughed and mocked me for saying that God was putting a vision in my spirit about opening a business with only $450.00 dollars. And the other guy was a rebel flag flying guy who first trained me when I came there. All of these guys I had an encounter with and it seemed like God was exiting them out for His own personal reasons. But for the rebel flag guy who wouldn't train or teach me everything, gave me an opportunity to get a promotion with his exiting.

Now remembering what my Supervisor told me, he will never allow me to be promoted as long as he is Supervisor. I saw an opportunity and I knew God gives favor and promotion in His will. I went straight to the top and requested for the job and the Plant manager gave me the job instantly. My Supervisor was so surprised but when God is in charge no one can predict your future. I ended up getting offered the job with extra money and a way to get off the shift with my old Supervisor. And out of all the drama I had on this shift, my mind goes back to the guy who God used to bring me back to myself. Who had informed me, I wasn't wrestling with flesh and blood but the wiles of the devil. After this test I learned a lot, one in particular was that God is a Sustainer. I thank God for keeping me from falling. He said in His Word in Ephesians 6:10-18 to be strong in the Lord and put on the whole armor of God, not a half armor but a whole armor. For we don't wrestle with flesh and blood but against principalities, against powers in high places, against the rulers of darkness of this age and against spiritual wickedness in the heavenly places. So can't you see what God is saying to us. He said stand and having done all to stand, stand even more. In this evil day keep your eyes, ears and heart open to God, by letting the Holy Spirit operate in you. You must die, your attitude, your personality and your understanding must change. And the only way for that to happen is to learn what God desires and what He don't desire. Learn His likes and dislikes. And let your character be made up through Jesus Christ and the Holy Spirit, which comes from God the Father.

A DREAM COME TRUE

Immediately after I had changed shifts, a man was drawn to me from God. I knew it, sometimes you just know it. Anyway, as I came back on the shift, I made myself comfortable. I knew almost everyone including the guy God sent to me. After working in the heat for so long, everyone would go outside on the porch to take a break to keep cool and sometimes I just sat and meditated by myself. There were picnic tables and benches on this porch where everybody gathered to smoke. One night, everyone went back before me and I just sat back and enjoyed the cool air and suddenly I was interrupted by this guy. Surprisingly, he asked me was I still serving the Lord as before? I told him yes, this is my life now and I wouldn't have it any other way. I told him if people could really grasped the great mysteries and revelations God has for us, they would be amazed and feel what I feel, illuminated. But these things are unseen because our understanding are blind until we come close to God in the Spirit. I told him about the Holy Spirit and why we all needed Him, because He is the one who reveals us to the Father.

The guy began telling me about himself, going to his mother's church and how much they were on fire for the Lord. He told me how close he came to going to the altar and accepting Jesus. He said, each time tears came flowing down his face but he couldn't get his legs to move forward and his mind would make it worst by telling him not to do it. I told him, God wanted him to make this perfect choice, just quit fighting it. Then he started confessing, asking me to promise not to tell anyone. So I promised not to tell, and he spoke out quietly telling me he couldn't get off drugs. Everytime he promised himself, he was through, he ended up right back doing it again. He said it was getting so bad that he was getting angry at his wife if she didn't help him get what he needed. He said, he went to the church on Sunday and was driven to "crack" on Thursday or Friday. "The more I wanted to stop, the eager I was to have it". I told him, I could identify with him because I've been in that same predicament before. Then he asked me how did you stop? I smiled and told him, "it's a long story but since you opened that door I'm dying to tell you because it's my testimony to guys like you and me". I was eager to tell him but I just gave him a brief consultation of my life. I even went back to when I first got Saved or accepted Christ. Then I immediately asked him did he want to accept Christ. And he said, no I'm not ready yet because I'm still drinking a lot of beer and amongst other things. I told him I accepted Christ and didn't know the real concept of accepting Him and I lived a life of pure'd hell. Otherwords, it seemed like hell broke loose when I accepted Christ. But now I see, I thank God for His keeping power because death was required of me a number of times but I really believed just because I was Saved, God prevented me from dying at them times. So I asked him again was he interested in accepting Christ and he said no he didn't want to rush in it to quick. But he told me he wanted help and wanted me to continue telling him my story.

So everyday, when I came to work he wanted to talk to me about something spiritual or about his problem. I gave him literature or pamphlets of the Word of God. He even asked for more literature because I had told him the more he fed himself with the Word the more he'll start understanding it better. He was really seeking for help to end his serious problem of drugs. He was a long haired pony tail, fat, hippy type fellow about thirty-five years old. Every time he told me about his mother's church and how much the Preacher and everybody there affected him, he got excited and happy. I told him the Holy Spirit was there in that church and He was after him. We prayed together on every occasion and he made sure of that because he came and got me everyday for prayer.

This went on for a couple of months until I heard a sermon from one of the Preachers saying, sometimes God will cut tides with someone you are working with so they want look to you all the time to be their god. So this last time we were together I was prompted to get to some serious business with him. It was time to cut the hanky panky, either you're in or you're not, I said to him. Then I told him God is desiring you to come to Him but you keep fighting it. You keep asking for prayer and you say tears rolls down your face at church, and something keep telling you to go to the altar but you holds back. I simply explained to him how the Holy Spirit works. I mean, I drilled into him that the Holy Spirit is like a real person, He's the One who keep trying to move you in the right direction. I said to him, I'm getting ready to release you because I don't want you to depend on me but the Holy Spirit, who is God. Either you accept Jesus tonight and get real with yourself and pray to God so your prayers can get heard or just keep fighting with yourself and losing the battle. The choice is yours, all I know its time for me to move on and let you depend on God. I have said and done all I can say and do.

Then I asked him after explaining the Holy Spirit to him, was he ready to accept Jesus as his Lord and Savior, and repent of his sins and turn from his wicked ways. He said yes, I guess I'm ready, I asked are you sure? He said yes I'm sure. So I recited the repentance prayer to him while he repeated after me. We were both teary eyed and we embraced each other afterwards. I insured him God will take it from there, in which He was already in charge anyway. I also warned him of satan and how he will try to come against him even more now. I told him satan was mad at me now but I didn't care because the most important thing is to help you get on the right side. I told him in Jesus name I rebuke satan because he already had attacked me twice when I brought his name up before and I don't want him to try it again, so I said, in Jesus name satan is mad at me. Right then, I remembered this christian guy had asked me a question and I answered in stupidity because I didn't know the Lord. But when I learned the Lord ways and got to know Him, I seen this christain guy again and I ran up to him to thank him and wanted him to see that I'm changed and full of the Holy Spirit. After this thought, I told my friend here, one day you'll see me again and will want me to see the Holy Spirit working in you. And this prophesy did come to pass but I'll get to it later in the chapter. I departed from him with confidence, knowing he was in God's hands now.

The very next day It was my mother's birthday and I had planned a day ahead what I wanted to do for her. It was something very special that I knew she would love. And I wanted to make her very happy, especially because of the great things she had been doing for me through the Lord. I was so happy this day on her birthday, I went early to get her a special gift and had a very special cake made and got her some flowers. She was gone from the house and this gave me a chance to sneak her gifts in the house to surprise her. My mother wasn't the only one up for a surprise this day. Little that I knew, the enemy was watching me and waiting for me to become off guard. And exciting as I was to surprise my mother, satan was more excited to surprise me. I see why Jesus kept telling His disciples, watch and pray, lest you enter into temptation, the spirit is willing but the flesh is weak. Even though, I told that guy who accepted Jesus, satan was mad at me now and I better use Jesus name to protect me from him(satan). I still fell the next day to watch and pray for God's protection. I took it for granted once more and let me tell you what happen. I had gotten my mother a kitten two years ago and his name was Blondie. He had grew to be a beautiful cat inside and out, he was just beautiful. And not only did my mother loved him but the whole family loved him.

That day when I came home with the gifts for my mother, Blondie was laying under my mother's car out of the hot sun. So I passed him and spoke to him and he just kept laying there. While I was in the house I received a phone call from my niece to pick up her kids from school for her. She said, she was with my mother at the hairdresser and wouldn't be finished in time to pick them up. And when I looked at the clock, I saw that I was running late, so I put a rush on what I was doing and dotted out the door running. I jumped in my vehicle and started it up and immediately put it in reverse. Once I put it in reverse, it felt like my brakes were still on or something was preventing me from going backwards. So I jumped out my vehicle to go around to see what it was holding me back and it was Blondie trying to get out from under my wheel. I pulled back up to let him out, and he crawled out unto the yard and I could tell damage had already happen. He was broken up inside his body and I was hysterical. I picked him up and put him in the back of my van, hoping I could save him. Even though, he was foaming at the mouth, I took off like a mad man, crying and praying that he will be okay. I was asking Blondie why did you come out from under mama's car and come under mine? I said why Blondie, why did you change? I kept driving and crying, when I got to the kid's school, I tried to hold my composure and wipe away my tears. But right away, my youngest grandniece asked me what was wrong and I hurried them in and told them I ran over Blondie and I'm trying to get him to a veterinarian. I told them to buckle up and I took off in a hurry but still trying to drive careful for them. My niece kept asking me questions about Blondie and I continued crying, but I apologized to them for crying in their presence and showing my weakness. I felt bad because they were getting weak and feeling sorrow because of me and I told them to be strong, but forgive me.

I finally arrived at the veterinarian office and I jumped out to get Blondie out and as I was reaching for him I noticed he wasn't breathing. My nephew asked, uncle Earl is he dead? I broke down considerably, carrying Blondie in my arms into the vet's office. I started confessing to the veterinarian what I did to him, crying and talking all the same time with tears flowing down my face. I told them I was trying to save him but he's dead, what do I do with him now? They told me they normally charge for disposing animals but in this case, they said don't worry we'll take care of it. I told them, I thank you all so much and I continued crying as I was walking out the door.

I jumped back in the van and drove off not knowing which way to go. I didn't want to go back to the house and face my mother so I headed toward my sister house, since I had her grandchildren with me anyway. When I arrived at my sister house, we got out and she immediately asked what was going on, after she seen our faces. Everybody tried to speak at one time, but I started reciting the whole story to her and her boyfriend. I broke down again after telling the story, saying it's mama's birthday and I wanted to make her happy but instead I'm going to make her sad by killing Blondie. And I kept crying that same sentence over and over again. I was so upset, my sister made me lay down in her spare bedroom. She brought me some aspirin trying to calm me down but I just kept crying and talking at the same time. Someone would asked why is he so upset, it was only a cat. At this time I didn't even know myself but one thing I did know, I loved that cat and I loved my mother even more. So I sobbed on that bed for an hour or more, then my brother-in-law asked me did I want a beer to calm me down. He told me, he wasn't trying to approach me the wrong way by offering me a beer but he thought it would help. I accepted and sure enough it did calm me down and after I was calmed, I got up, still in a daze, wondering what was happening.

After I was calmed, the Holy Spirit reminded me right away of what I told the fellow on my job about the devil being mad at me for praying and helping him come to the knowledge of God and pronouncing him in the kingdom in Jesus name. I was reminded then of satan trying to steal my joy. And being shame to say, he did, yes he(satan) succeeded for that moment. My feelings was tore up, I was bent out of shape and I didn't want to see my mother's face when she heard of it. Our feelings and emotions do flare up in situations sometimes uncontrollable. But I thank God for the Holy Spirit who reminds us of all things and God's son Jesus Christ, who we can go to freely under any circumstances and open up to Him. I explained to my sister and everybody what was going on with me. It was a testimony for me and I gave God the glory. Even when satan throws his hardest blows on us, it may seem unbearable sometimes but if we just stand and know God is there, He said, He will never leave us nor forsake us. And just don't let satan keep beating you down.

Now the weekend had passed, I got over that experience, thanks to the Lord. It was a new week at work, it seemed like God had me on a whole different journey. I had already released the guy I had helped in Jesus name. As I said before, the Holy Spirit had pointed out to me through a sermon I heard to move on and let him seek God for himself or he would be depending on me instead of God. But I had to tell him what happen to me over the weekend. After telling him, he laughed and I told him this thing is more serious than what you think. It's real and this battle is between God and satan and we are in the middle. The more we lean on God side, satan gets mad and the more we lean on his(satan) side he gets glad.

Time was going on and I was doing quite a lot of overtime, trying to save money to get out on my own, once again. I had to continue to ask God to give me patience because I would repeatedly jump ahead of God on major decisions and it would cost me deeply. So I tried practicing patience a lot, for the very reason, once I get an idea I allowed my anxiety to take over me. On one of the shifts I was working overtime on, I ran into a fellow who I used to deal with in the streets. He asked me, why are you working so much overtime? I answered him with a smile, "I'm broke, I need money". He replied, "you know how to come up, you know how you used to do it". Then he replied again, you don't have to be broke. Still smiling, I told him that life is behind me now. Plus, I'm in too deep, God have shown me too much now. Still smiling, I told him this thing I'm in, is kind of like the Mafia. When you're in too deep with the Mafia and try to get out, you have to fear your life. Well, that's the way I feel now, if I go back into the world with all this knowledge God patiently gave me, I feel like my life will be taken. I love this life better anyway and I know God will see that I prosper. I said to him, you need to come and try it because it is much peaceful once you get to know and understand the Lord ways and His Word. Then he laughed and told me he went to this church with his mother and people were falling on the floor and making noises. He said that's not for me, to me it seems too hypocritical, it's too many hypocrites in the church. I smiled and went on my way with nothing else to say. Then two days later the Holy Spirit spoke to me about this hypocritical matter for this fellow. The Holy Spirit prompted me to go and tell him what He placed in my mind. And the amazing thing about it was, the Holy Spirit arranged for us to meet right back in the same spot alone. I brought the hypocritical matter back to his attention. I said to him, you know when you told me the people of the church were hypocrites, well, the Holy Spirit open my eyes to you. I began telling him my story; when I was out there in the world doing my thing to the fullest, I didn't even know about christians, not only thinking about them. I was too much into me and what I was doing, I didn't have time to think about anyone else, satan had my mind so much. Now, I'm sitting here listening at you calling church folks hypocrites, no you're the hypocrite in the world. Because if you was true to the world, you wouldn't even think of church folks, you wouldn't have time. So God is pricking your heart to consider talking about church folks, so quit fighting it and come and join us on this side. He smiled and said, boy you are something else. I smiled and said no, it's not me, it's God in me and he went on.

I was bumping into people constantly, one after another on my job. One of the guys I had been studying the Word with kept stopping me as we were changing shifts. He kept asking me about us going in business together. We had spoking earlier about different businesses and shared some information on each of our ideas. He was temporarily in a construction business so he was telling me he knew about having a business. I told him I never thought of joining up with anybody unless they were understandable about this being God's project and not ours. I mentioned, I had to pray about us joining together, then I took him to scripture reminding him of Achan of Joshua 7:19,20 and how he accursed Israel by taking something he shouldn't have. I let him know, if God grant someone with me, he has to be truthful also. He went on to tell me about this building in his hometown that was vacant and was exactly what we needed so he urged me to go look at it. I asked myself what is going on? Is God sending this guy to me or is he someone who want a piece of the pie. I went to prayer about this situation and asked God to show me or give me a sign, if I shall trust this guy. While waiting on my answer from God, I thought I would take a ride down to where this place was. And as I was riding I couldn't help for thinking about the old days, when I had started a business in this same town before. Finally, I arrived at the place and it was the place my Supervisor was talking about. But this time I got out and looked the place over. It had a lot of potential with two buildings in one. One had been a hotdog and hamburger stand and the other building, a store and poolroom, in which both were joined together with a door to go side to side. My imagination of a fish market and a restaurant were more in view with this place. Just a different location than I had in mind, but the more I thought about it the more anxious I became. I kept reflecting back to the building back in my hometown and thinking about how much work I would have to do there. And also sizing up this building and location to see which would be better.

While contemplating on this amazing thought, I was still doing the work of a disciple, trying to win souls to Christ. During the shift change I was at my locker and this same guy came up to ask me did I go down there and look at the place. I said, yes I did and it had great potential. He suggested that we should go further to find out how much the rent would be. Then he went on to tell me about this guy who used to work for him and how he was demanding for his back pay he owed him. He told me this former employee of his was nagging and worrying him about his pay. Then he told me he went and prayed to God about the situation and he asked God to take care of this situation and remove him from his life. He said guess what happen, I said what! He said the guy got killed and now I don't have to worry about him anymore, he laughed about the situation with gladness. He said, God took care of him for me, immediately I was stunned, and discernment came in my spirit causing me to ask him, "did you pray for him to die"? He told me, smiling, saying it was something like that, then he said, he just asked God to remove him. And not only that, he said he did this before with some of his family members, praying that they be removed and they died. I was puzzled and deep inside I didn't think this was Christ like. I told him you just don't pray for people to have any hardship or death. He felt my concern but said King David prayed against people in the Bible. He then felt remorsed and said he will try to go and see the family of this guy and speak with his wife. The next day, he told me he left the guy's wife some money and would pay her the rest he owed.

Right then, I knew this guy had knowledge of the Bible and could speak in tongues, but lacked the love of Christ in him. We all say we love Jesus Christ with our lips but when you truly love Jesus Christ, you gain a heart of Christ. You begin to feel what He feel about everything and everybody. The love He(Jesus) has is suppose to rest inside of us, which surpasses all understanding and knowledge. Otherwords, when you live in true love unconditional, as God's love, He gives you a supernatural eye to see people as He sees them. When you have this supernatural eye, you have the supernatural discernment to speak to someone in God's voice and actions. You'll speak the words God want you to speak to help another. After seeing what I've saw in this guy, who I'll call Ron, I couldn't help for thinking, is this what happens to christians after being a christian a long period of time. Do you really lose your zeal for working in God's kingdom? Do you just start living like regular folks? I mean, I don't know, I'm just wondering, I'm a beginner at this and I'm fired up for the Lord. To me I thought once you are fired up for the Lord, it lasts forever! But now I'm having second thoughts. But I thank God for showing me His great mysteries and great revelations to keep me from falling into patterns men makes.

Later God enabled me to see a friend of mine at his place of business. This friend had been in a similar predicament like mine, being busted for drugs and turning his life around through the Grace of God. To make a long story short, when I finally saw him again, he was a minister in his church and right then at lunch time he took his employees by the hands and asked if I wanted to join and I did. He prayed a long hearty prayer and we talked afterwards about his change. And he was fired up for the Lord and full of joy. He told me he haven't slowed down since the first day he turned his life to God twenty years ago. This gave me so much joy to see, I said to myself, this is the way I want to be forever fired up for the Lord.

Now I had two thoughts that came to my mind about Ron. For one, he had the knowledge of God but not the heart of Christ. As it says in the scripture 2 Timothy 3:5, having a form of godiness but denying the power. And from such people turn away. The other thought was, should I leave him alone or try to help him get his zeal back for God to do service for Him. Achan, from the scriptures came to my remembrance again so I prayed to God again to show me a sign because I was getting confused on my judgment on this guy. And all the time God had answered my prayers about this guy, Ron. But I wasn't aware of it because deep down inside I wanted him to be the one to go in business with because of the convenience. So I blocked the signs God showed me of Ron with my own anxiety and ignorance.

So I went ahead and took a chance with him and the first thing for us to do were to contact the man who was renting the buildings. My desires started overflowing my thoughts, where I couldn't see nothing but my desires. As the scripture says in Psalms 37:4 delight yourself also in the Lord, and He will give you the desires of your heart. But I didn't witness this scripture at all, instead, the scripture I acknowledged in this process that I was headed for was in Psalms 145:19, which states, He will fulfill the desires of those who fear Him; He also will hear their cry and save or rescue them. Sometimes God will fulfill your desires even if they get to heavy for you that you have to cry to be rescued.

So we met the man who owned the buildings and he walked us through the buildings. The bigger one, which I dreamed of putting the fish market was in bad shape but the small one was much better. The man quoted the price on each building. The large building he wanted $650.00 a month and on the smaller one he wanted $350.00 a month and for both he wanted $800.00 a month. I had my mind on the fish market but Ron had his mind on the restaurant. Neither one of us had the money for either one. We told the man of the building to give us a few days to decide what to do. These buildings had been vacant for four years. Ron came to me at work asking me what have I came up with. I told him I was still trying to figure out how to get the whole thing. Then Ron suggested that we should get the restaurant for $350.00 and see what we can do with it, plus he said don't despise small beginnings. I paused for a few minutes, smiled and said, I think it is a brilliant idea. We called the man and set up another appointment to meet him out there to make a deal with the restaurant. The man wanted $350.00 for the first month and $350.00 deposit. And the sad part about it was, we didn't have but $175.00 a piece so we had to ask the man could we pay the deposit later. Plus, we asked him to give us a extra month or two before starting monthly payments. He agreed and we signed the lease and Ron and I was partners now. Now I remind you, earlier in the previous chapters, I was made a mockery of by saying to some guys, God was putting in my spirit to start a business with only four hundred and fifty dollars. But God is real!

The journey had now begun with our crazy faith, trusting God for everything. While I was working twelve hour night shifts, Ron was working twelve hour day shifts. We were off on the same days until Ron decided to quit work to go do his side business of contracting and preparing the restaurant, in which we would meet up and discuss daily. I came into this business expecting God to give us favor for His glory, not ours. My hopes were very high, even though, I didn't have any money, my expectancy of God was deep. That's why I didn't want to get connected up with anybody seeking their own glory. I knew from the bottom of my heart, what ever it was to do with this business, God had to be the center and get the glory. We didn't have a dime after we paid the down payment. You talking about scratch, this is what you call starting from scratch.

This story came to my mind that described my character. Scientist were doing a test on some boys to see how they were to react. They put a poor optimistic boy in a room full of cow manure up to his waist with a shovel. And they put a rich pessimistic boy in a room full of toys. The scientist watched them for an hour or two. After an hour the rich pessimistic boy was sitting in the middle of the room with a sad, ungrateful look on his face. And the poor optimistic boy was throwing cow manure over his shoulder with the shovel, laughing and having a lot of fun. The scientist were confused, they couldn't figure out why the optimistic boy was so happy in all that cow manure. And the pessimistic boy were so sad with everything a boy could want. So the scientist asked the pessimistic boy why was you so sad and he proclaimed, he was bored and there wasn't anything there that could make him happy. Then they asked the optimistic boy, why was you so happy in there with all that manure. The optimistic boy replied, out of all this stuff, something good is bound to be under the bottom. The rich pessimistic boy had everything in his room and he didn't have anything to look forward to or hope for. The poor optimistic boy kept hope in his heart no matter what the circumstance was. I was like that optimistic boy, a prisoner of hope and I thank God for this hope. Some people are well off or rich in their finances, through their family history and can't seem to understand why Preachers preach on wealth, hope and faith for us to come one of these days. And why people believe in these sayings and preaching, Jesus Himself recited in Luke 4:18,19; The Spirit of the Lord is upon Me, because he anointed Me to preach the Gospel to the poor;

He has sent Me to heal the brokenhearted, to proclaim liberty to the captives and recovery of sight to the blind, to set liberty to those who are oppressed and to proclaim the acceptable year of the Lord. So this is why we believe in these Preachers because we believed in Jesus Christ and His Word.

I noticed my partner hadn't grasped the full insight of this hope and the glory of the God. He came to me with assurance of a financial ability to set us free, to move us up to the next level. He told me don't worry, he'll take care of everything because of the contracts he'll be getting from his jobs. I told him I'll do the best I can out of my weekly checks to meet him halfway. But I knew, God had control over this whole situation and not him. I still agreed with him to kick start this business so we could get up and running. A few days later he came to me with his head hanging down and looking sad, I asked him what was the matter? Then he told me, the deal fell through so he wouldn't be able to jump start the business like he thought. I was calm because deep down inside I knew it was God stepping in to cease his deals. For there was no one to get the glory from this but God, not even me. We began making preparations for the restaurant, we both were full of joy, knowing we were on the way now. We first took up the old carpet and bought paint to paint the concrete floor. Then we hired a couple of fellows from catchout corner, a place where guys need jobs to make it for a moment, they painted the walls. We went halfway on everything, it was times when I didn't have any money and it was times when he didn't neither, then we took turns spending.

I was still trying to get it together to get my own place to live. My mother helped me a lot, even though I was paying my way to live there. She continued to go out of her way to help me get back on feet. She was very understanding about the things I was doing, it's nothing like a mother's love. No matter what I went through she was always there by my side. It reminded me of the movie THE PASSION OF CHRIST. No matter what they did to Jesus Christ, His mother was right by His side all the way unto death. By watching this kind of love, unconditional love brings tears to my eyes. I truly believe God put this kind of love in a woman in Genesis 3:15 quoting; And I will put enmity between you(satan) and the woman, and between your seed and her seed. I truly believe God gave a woman a part of Him, this unconditional love for her child, so satan wouldn't be able to deceive her of her Seed. From Genesis 3:15 to Revelation 12, I believed satan came after Mary through King Herod in Matthew 2:7-23 to destroy the male child, Jesus. And because of the love God placed in the woman for her child, Jesus was saved, amongst God's exceeding power and Angels. So I thank God for this unconditional love He placed in a mother for her child. This is the kind of love I wished could be in my heart, and all men toward our children. This is how God love His children, even though, we were deep in our sins and not worthy of Him, He sent His only begotten Son to redeem us from our sins and to reconcile us to Him. Not only His Son but He sent the Holy Spirit also to cleanse us, to guide us and to remind us of Him. If this is not love, even Jesus said in His words in John 15:13 greater love has no one than this, than to lay down One's life for His friends.

I paused from the restaurant scene for a minute or two, to tell you how things were turning right here in the middle of this whole process. Through God I was handed $1500.00 dollars to put down on a house. First there was my driving license, which had seemed hopeless, but I was able through God's help to accomplish driving license. At this time I remembered when I told myself coming out that courtroom after looking at all the judgments against me, that it seemed impossible to turn everything around. The Holy Spirit right away reminded me, being with God nothing is impossible, so I smiled and shook my head. And here it was now, I'm getting a house, it seemed unbelievable but it happen. So now here I was with an automobile payment, a house payment and a restaurant on the way, all staring me in the face. Besides getting the restaurant prepared, I had to get my house prepared with furniture. I had none whatsoever but it was a thrill just knowing that I was finally able to own my own house again and put a roof over my daughters head. A place she can call her own, I thanked God over and over again. With concentrating on all of the transitions, I really depended on God to help me out. Oh yeah, in the midst of all this, I also changed churches, trying to go where my girlfriend was going and plus, to be fed more spiritual food. This was really a transitional move for me and I needed a spiritual father for right now advice.

My friend Mike was congratulating me for the house and also telling me, "now you are going to see the real deal". You will be on your own and not under your mother. Then he said in so-called sympathy, this will be the test, If you can stay off crack. You want have your mother there to govern you, he retorted. I was kind of surprised to hear this, even though satan had already approached me in this area of my mind. Right away I said to myself how many people are counting on me to fall or betting on me to lose. It could've as well been amongst my family also. But God already had it planned out for me because the house was twenty or thirty minutes from any familiarity and remain that way as of today. My family and friends asked me why did I move so far, practically in another town.

But as the days were going on, time were seemly speeding up, I guess because of the transitions I was making in my life. I was very excited, but at the same time I knew I had to stay close to the Lord. During the four years I stayed locked in God's Word I became rooted. I felt like the first three verses in Psalms 1 was for me, which states: Blessed is the man who walks not in the counsel of the ungodly, nor stands in the paths of sinners, nor sits in the seat of the scornful. But his delight is in the law of the Lord, And in His law he meditates day and night, he shall be like a tree planted by the rivers of water, that brings forth it's fruit in it's season, whose leaf also shall not wither, and whatever he does shall prosper. Up to this point, I had been learning much as I could learn of the Father, the Son and the Holy Spirit and of witnessing. Soaking in as much as I could soak in. Otherwords I ate, slept and lived the Word. God was preparing me for a "ride", I wouldn't have ever been able to handle, without His Word. He was getting ready to take me to another dimension or level in His ministry because of my own faults, just to show me myself even closer.

The restaurant was coming alive again after four years of standing. My partner and I stood back after the painting were done and saw a future. So we did what was next and that was to hit the pavement to do the paperwork. We went downtown to see the people who was responsible for helping us do things legitimate. One thing I did learn in this small town, everybody knew everybody from childhood. We got more favor and cooperation from the town because of my partner's family name. The fire chief and other important men joked with my partner about his daddy and their football experience. We had a few obstacles, they pointed out to us after inspecting the building. But thanks be to God, we prayed and God gave us wisdom to fixed it. So we had our paperwork altogether and was ready to rock and roll or get the ball bouncing. Now it was time for us to get some equipment. But guess what, we didn't have any money to go any further, we said to ourselves, we're stuck. And right at this time, a restaurant was closing across town and ready to sell their equipment, which were exactly what we needed. The most amazing thing I've ever seen was how God moves in your behalf before you even think or asked. And when you see God moving in your life supernaturally, He's showing you His face to let you know how real He is. And when God shows you His face, it reflects so much excitement, you can't take it all. You will no longer praise Him with your lips but you'll praise Him with all your heart, with all your mind and all your soul.

I had been looking at Bishop T.D. Jakes and a few more on Television at their schedule times. And T.D. Jakes spoke a word weeks before we even thought about opening the restaurant. This sermon stayed in my spirit, which T.D. Jakes quoted, "When God gives you favor". He said, sometimes if you're having financial problems in your business, God will send somebody to help you and give you money and they want be worrying you to pay them back or try to receive the glory for what they've done. One day, I was in the driveway of my friend Mike, telling him of our problem with the progress of the restaurant. Mike called me almost everyday to check on our progress. So he asked me what are you all going to do about getting some money to move forward. I told him about the word I got from a sermon Bishop T.D. Jakes was preaching. I told Mike, at this time I couldn't go on anything but faith. I truly believed what I've heard from the Bishop will come to pass. So my partner Ron and I had to pause for a while until we came up with the funds to move forward. Ron assured me by saying, don't worry I've been doing a job for these guys who buy old houses and fixed them up and resale them. I'll make enough money to get us to the next level. But God had other plans, and when God has other plans, believe me it comes to pass. God wants the glory and He knows our hearts. When Ron came to me to tell me something went wrong again, with confusion all over his face, I knew it was the Lord stepping in. I had already been in deep prayer to God about this situation.

A few days later, out of the clear blue, Ron told me the guys he was working for asked how were we doing with the restaurant? They told Ron if we needed any kind of assistance let them know. Ron said he didn't like accepting loans from anybody. I was so amused about hearing this offer, I almost burst. I started explaining to Ron about the word God gave me through Bishop T.D. Jakes, I replied, this is it. This is God delivering His Word to us in action. My partner kept saying I just don't know. I tried to convince him that God haven't brought us this far to leave us. He said, he'll arrange a meeting for us to come together to discuss it. I kept feeding Ron's mind with positive hope as though we already had the help, so we prepared ourselves to ask for twenty-five hundred dollars. We came together and they asked us what were our plans. We told them we wanted to start a franchise with the business, in which we were very serious about a franchise. Note: we didn't have a clue of experience in the restaurant business but through faith we thought we could take it to the highest limit. Then they went on to tell us to let them meditate on it. These guys were men of God also, and I'm sure they had to go to God about this situation! After a few days, Ron told me they okayed it and they will be here the next day with the money. They came and we all sat down and went over the contract they had made stating the amount we borrowed. They then said if we ever become a franchise they would like 2% of the earnings. But they never put a limit of time on the money and when this happened I couldn't hold it. I had to call my friend Mike to remind him of the time I told him of the word I received from God through Bishop T.D. Jakes came to pass. I told Mike of the two guys that visited us with the money and they didn't think anything else about it, just like I told him. He was amazed and he said he do believe God will move in your behalf if you have faith.

We went straight across town to the restaurant that was closing to negotiate some deals with some equipment. We bought tables, chairs and booths that seated at lease thirty-two to thirty-four people, which filled us up. We received a few more items from this owner for a very good price. We went elsewhere and found a pressure deep fryer, a stove with a grill on top of it, a three component sink to wash our pans in and two frigidares and two freezers, in which two were gave to us. God gave us favor in working with the hearts of these people. It was like every move we were making God was right there seeing things through. It gave me so much confidence to know, we have a God who never leave us nor forsake us. We had all necessities for the restaurant put in their proper places and was now ready for the final inspections. We heard, the inspector who was coming was very thorough and didn't play no games. We tried to make sure everything were in proper conditions. When he arrived he went over the place like a fine tooth comb. He was calling out and writing down stuff that needed improvement. And that was fine but when he mentioned, we couldn't open because of a small matter. I burst out to my partner saying, "the devil is a liar", we came to far not to open, then I repeated, the devil is a lie. And immediately, the inspector said while still writing, but I guess you all can open and I'll come back and see have you all corrected these problems. Plus I'll give you all a high rating to go down in the next paper. We thanked him so much for his help. He left and Ron and I gave each other a high-five while laughing about the out burst I made of the devil. Ron said, he drawed up in a knot. We knew from here, we were on our way.

We had only one problem left, we had spent everything we had and couldn't get any grocery to move to the next level. So we both thought about the guys who lended us the money before. We discussed it again and again trying to build our nerves up to ask. Ron made a lot of sense when he said, we asked too low, we should have asked for more. I said yeah, you're right, that's why we are going to ask for more, so we agreed. They came to the rescue once more, which moved us to another level to open the doors. We were now prepared for business, except for cooks. We had a so-called professional came by to check us out. We were already using Ron's children and kinsfolk in the kitchen. When the professional cook saw the set-up, he worked for one or two days and decided this wasn't what he was looking for.

He couldn't see the dream we had and starting from ground level just wasn't what he was looking for. So he told us he had to quit and we respected that and went on with the business.

We had some of the communities coming in trying our food, black and white people. Ron's kinsmen had worked in some fast food restaurants so that helped out a lot because our business was set-up for fast food anyway. We sold hamburgers and hotdogs, but our specialty were chicken and fish. We were set-up to sell from two piece snack boxes to family size meal boxes of chicken and fish. I really personally wanted to sell strictly fish and shrimp and open up the building next door to make it out of a fish market. But my partner wanted a chicken fast food restaurant, so we named the restaurant Chicken Of The Sea. We came together on reasonable prices, in which I checked out a few prices around the vicinity. Ron was a high dollar man, by this I mean he always told me not to be scared to charge higher prices. And I always liked to be as reasonable as I could, maybe sometimes too low. It was like we were looking at the glass differently, either half full or half empty. So we had to come to an agreement with the prices. It was like he was greedy and I wasn't greedy enough. But anyway we got settled and was drawing a little business now. We put up a big advertise sign up in front of the building and went all over town spreading the news by word of mouth. And a few more people were calling in for orders.

Ron was seeing the business picking up and sure enough, when I came in one morning he had faxed some of our regular customers all over town the new prices he had made himself. They were two dollars more on everything. I asked him what in the world are you doing. He said we had the prices too low and he wanted to try it his way. I couldn't believe it, I was stunned and speechless because everything were priced with the surroundings. I went along with it just to let him see the outcome. So we waited and waited for customers to come in. Even the walk-ins had seemly seized. Then after a week with merely no business, he came to me and told me, I think that was a bad idea raising the prices, maybe you was right. I explained to him that it's better to sell in volume than unit. He listened and agreed that we go back to reasonable prices. But the damage was already done and we had to come up with a plan to get people to come back in again. And right here, little that I knew, I was in for the "ride" of my life.

We had to go back into deep prayers to ask God for divine favor and direction. Then we thought of some of the Plants that surrounded us. We had flyers of lunch specials made and sent them to just some of the work places in the area. Ron had spoke earlier about us not having the employment to handle the large orders if they hit us. But at this point he was ready to take the chance. And sure enough, these Plants were calling us all at once with orders to large to be filled. We hustled to get the orders out and we made some mistakes and lost some customers. And it really hurt us on the ones we lost, they didn't have the time to be delayed, so some wouldn't take a chance on us again. Ron was right on this ordeal about us not being able to handle the large orders. But even through this ordeal, we started new business with some. It was just enough for us to work on our perfection. That deep prayer with God really poured it on, more than we could handle. God had blessed us with a legitimate full scale restaurant right in the middle of the suburbs, the rural and the interstate. God was working it out every step of the way. He was making something out of nothing and it was all for His glory.

THE RIDE

I was still working at the job where me and my partner met. I was working twelve hour night shifts and when I got off work I wouldn't miss a morning from going to the restaurant. My partner had quit the job and was running the restaurant with his family and doing his contracting business on the side. So I was pulling my shift at the restaurant as well, regardless of the lack of sleep I was getting. I was very dedicated to everything I started and took it very serious. Even though, I was putting a lot of time in the restaurant, I knew I had to keep my job in order to pay on my newly bills, I had created. At the time, I didn't realize how critical things could be, during this transition with everything being new to me. Then all of a sudden, it seemed like an Angel came down from heaven to give us an extra boost at the restaurant. I supposed it was an Angel or it could have been something else. First, a poolroom moved in next door and started a nightclub on the weekend. We were totally against it at first until we realized we could draw a lot of business from them. We were generating a nice amount of money from the poolroom. We didn't like the idea of it but it was nothing we could do about it at this time. But we were very careful from falling into temptation with these guys because my partner knew them and they were making themselves right at home in our place.

Now I want to pause right here for a moment. During this time here I was also witnessing on my job to people God put in my path. This particular middle aged guy was drawn to me by God. He was on first shift and I was on third shift but Ron, my partner, had been working him on some of his contracting jobs. So I actually got to know him for the first time when he came off one of the jobs Ron had him on. He was at the restaurant and needed a way home so Ron asked if I could drop him off on the way home and I agreed. At this time, I didn't know God was setting me up to witness because it was the farthest thing on my mind here at the restaurant. I didn't know anything about him and he didn't know anything about me neither. So we went most of the way with little to say to each other. And about halfway to where he was living, which was at a rehabilitation housing for ex-convicts and ex-drug users, in which I didn't know at that time.

But anyway he started opening up to me about his problems and his past, which involved abusing drugs. He kept telling me he didn't like going home because it was too much temptation and it was hard for him to reject all the time. Then he said, it was good to be here in this town around people he didn't know. I just listened to his cry and plea of a struggling soul who would like to escape, but didn't know how. And he kept wrestling with the same problem over and over again until it became a lifestyle, hoping one day it would change for a better life. You see it, but you can't seem to reach it. Happiness and joy inexpressibly with all wisdom and understanding is only through one door. Which seems so hard, so thick and so difficult, that the journey seems better going backwards than going forward through that open door. And everytime you fall down or get knocked down you want to give up but something inside of you keep making you get up and try it again. Why do we try over and over again? When we look back from where we came, then see where we have come, then maybe we do see a little hope. A little hope is better than none because once you have accomplished a little hope then that makes you want to go further to a bigger hope. And when God is in your corner and you are in His chamber, the bigger hopes becomes more clearer and more willing to go forward. Then the thickness, the difficulties and the hard and troublesome paths becomes minor. Therefore, we goes through that door with expectancy of a new future and a new drive to continue to go on, no matter what should get in our way. We wake up wanting something new to happen in our lives and we continue running and running toward the prize until we can't run anymore. I advise anybody, not to give up and become complacent with their lives, but to push on to gain Godly wisdom above man's wisdom and seek understanding and love for yourself so God's perfect plan can draw you nearer to the reason you're here.

I continued listening to him until it was time for me to collaborate on the same problems I had went through myself. After opening up on just some of my testimonies and past incidents, he was amazed. He didn't have a clue, I was there once before too. Evidently, he didn't know I was a man of God until he sensed, I was professing how God delivered me and pulled me out of the horrible pit of drugs and drug abuse and other terrible things. Then he asked, how did we get on this subject? I told him, I don't go around telling people I'm in God but when you open that door for me to come in, I couldn't resist it. Simply, because I know when God draws someone to me that has experienced the same lifestyle as I had, and I know this is the ministry and the work God has for me, so I let it go. I dropped him off at the rehabilitation place where he was living, with both of us in joyable spirits.

The very next two days he was working on the same shift I was. I already knew it wasn't a coincident for us meeting but I didn't know God had other plans. I was the leadsman at the time on my shift and he came to work with me on the floor to help me out. He still had a little wildness in him and he joked around a little, and come to find out we were the same age. It was like God had planted him there for me to tutor him into sincerity of the Lord. He took the Word lightly but I was serious about the Word because I knew how satan was out to deceive and trick us back into bondage of drug addiction, and satan knew just how to do it. So right away, this guy came to me continuously in every situation concerning the job and he asked for advice for everything, and God stepped in on every occasion. Even when he had job related problems and he couldn't fix it, God blessed me to make it seem simple. And each time he said, you think you can fix everything and I explained to him, it wasn't me, it was God showing me favor. I tried to tell him when you are obedient to God and serious or sincere with Him, then God will show favor in the small and in the big things. Then God put it in my spirit to teach him everything I knew and he was a faithful student. He ran my job like a champ and was the least one to get my job because where he was coming from. I spoke with sincerity to the Supervisor, telling him if I go on vacation he would be the man to handle my job but the Supervisor said, that's not possible. And little that I and the Supervisor knew, I was leaving for good and this guy was the one to get my job. Jumping from $6.00 per hour on a temp job to $10.00 dollars an hour on a full-time job, and I was very happy for him. We never know what God has in store for our lives. That's why I loved to witness when someone was drawn to me from God. It wasn't like a job or duty but it was more like an excitement to be able to share God's experience in my life to others.

But as the restaurant was coming more and more into view, my mind was getting more and more on the restaurant. We had Ron's family working in the restaurant because it was too far for my family to travel. At first, I kind of struggled with that because satan was trying to put thoughts in my mind, but I immediately exited the thought out of my mind so we could go on with our plans. Because, if it hadn't been for his family working almost for free I don't know what we would have done. We couldn't afford any cooks yet, and it's a shame to say, neither one of us really knew how to cook and we really didn't have plans to cook. But the restaurant was up and running and we had the name put on the window, CHICKEN OF THE SEA. Believe it or not people were wondering what in the world this name was about. I used to tell them my partner loved chicken and I loved fish and shrimp so we crossed the name up. God was really in this place, His glory was all in it. We were sitting in the middle of God's glory and didn't even realize it. Everything just fell in place, whatever was next to do was done, if it were our doing or not it was done. Ron and I were knit together in doing everything, we had customers he knew in the town coming in, and between the poolroom and the Plant workers, we were beginning to do alright with our finances. I was still anxious to move faster but Ron wanted us to take our time because of the workers we had and it did make a lot of sense. Even though, I was still coming up with ideas to advertise to attract more business, I had to place them on the back burner and practice more patience.

All of a sudden, out of the clear blue my oldest daughter visited us to try our food and to see what her daddy had accomplished. I was so glad she came and she was the first of my family to come and see what I was doing. She didn't come alone, literally speaking, she came with some good news for Ron and I, which we called, news from an Angel. After she ate and complemented our food, telling us how good it was, she mentioned to us how restaurants came to her job to set up as vendors to sell lunch. She gave us the number to call for our contact person, she also told us that they had a spot open on Wednesdays. We prayed about it and were already excited as though we knew we were going to get the spot. We called and set an appointment up with the contact person. I went over to meet her and we went over the menu, then we discussed the prices and came to an agreement. We got the spot and we had two weeks to get it together. Now I was putting twelve hours in at work and eight hours a day at the restaurant. Ron and his family tried to run me home on several occasions to get some rest. But I was determined to get the restaurant headed toward the right direction. Sometimes I have a tendency to drive hard until everything is in place and running smooth. I have a strong determination to try to make things around me concerning work or business run correctly and excellent, above measure. At times I've allowed things to burn me out or I've gotten depressed because it wasn't done soon enough. And I know that's not right in the sight of God so I have to constantly pray to be able to hold my composure and trust Him more.

Our first day as a job vendor was a success and a new beginning for Ron and I. The next day while I was at work, Ron showed up to give me some more good news. He proclaimed to me that we might could become a vendor at another Firm bigger than the one we had. He said, "they also have an opening on a opposite day", I jumped to the ceiling with excitement. Ron and I were seeing big things and were excited together again as if we already had it. I knew God was on the move blessing us to higher levels and giving us a way to support the restaurant to higher horizons. We both went to the presentation that the contact lady had set up for us. We had to bring one of our favorite entrees to some of the consultants of the Firm to test out. They all tasted the entrees and looked at each other with amazement, licking their fingers and lips giving us two thumbs up and was signing us up for the following week. Things were looking up for us, we had two vendors a week at major Firms with about three to four hundred people to feed. It was time to get busy cooking, in which Ron and I had to learn quickly, mostly from his wife and my mother. We moved from a whole new level of cooking, from fast foods to full course meals. We went to this new Firm and ended up with a good amount of money as well as expected. We both were so excited, thanking and praising the Lord every step of the way.

But the only thing I failed to do was check with God before I made this major move in my life that probably changed my whole view of life. I had gotten so excited, I left my job and went into the business full-time. Not thinking if the business could support my bills and finances, but taking one of the biggest chances of my life. I didn't give it a second thought because business was going so good. So now we were operating the restaurant, getting a flow from it with the poolroom next door and with other local people also. Plus serving twice a week to two of the largest Firms from 11:00am to 3:00pm. I was looking at this as an opportunity for Ron and I to keep our bills up at home and at the restaurant. I had to be really focused on everything now, which was probably a big mistake for me leaving my job. But I wasn't looking at that anymore, I was looking straight ahead. My partner didn't like it at all but I'll explain it later. He was already struggling with his bills at home and I knew if I didn't do some deep concentrating, I was going to be the next to have problems. But God was good and is always good. He blessed us with another major Firm to feed on a different day from the other ones. They all were lined up perfectly through God's grace. I knew it had to be God because everything lined up to perfectly. We got in the kitchen and stirred up some meals, something we realized we couldn't brag or boast about in our name. We made these meals, took them to these places, hoping they would be good. The people loved the food so much they wanted to come to the restaurant. I knew in my heart they loved us for bringing such good food. I told my partner, Ron, God has really blessed this food with His anointing. It's His doings and hands in the food that makes it so good. We had to laugh to ourselves with such joy, saying this is one thing we can't brag on because we were not cooks.

Ron was telling me he was thinking about hiring this middle age woman to help us out on deliveries and a little in the kitchen, but first we had to fit her into our budget. I had come up with a plan for us to pay ourselves and I presented it to Ron. This was the time we were beginning to know each other very well and on a whole new level or perspective. When money comes on the scene we tend to change or become a person of another dimension, something like a Dr. Jekyll, Mr. Hyde kind of person. Anyway, after presenting my plan to him, he was in a whole new personality. He told me, he couldn't see any way we could pay our home bills with any of the money we were making. Then he said to me, "you should have stayed on your job, I have the contracting business to fall back on". He went on to say, we needed to open an account to save up money for the restaurant and it's future. He probably was right about everything he just said but at this particular time I didn't want to hear it. The first thing that came to my mind was how he was already struggling financially because he was believing God was meaning for him to endure affliction. But I refused to lose anything God had gave me, I came too far and God had been too good to me to go backwards. I knew I left my job too soon by not checking with the Holy Spirit first. And Ron wasn't letting it die, he kept repeating it to me about leaving my job. The statements dug into my soul even more, almost like hot coals pressed against me. But regardless of my mistake, I was still refusing to go backwards. That's why, I came up with a plan that would help the both of us.

But evidently, he explained that it was purposeful for him to go through suffering from God at this time, and I had a totally different aspect of life. I had heard Prophetess Anita Bynum preached a word from God, saying it was purposeful for her to reach the other side and this was a death walk for her. Otherwords, I took it like I had to make it, I couldn't go back. It was a matter of life or death if I didn't press forward. I told my partner we had two different views on life and I couldn't settle for his view. Right then, we developed a separation with each other. God was putting everything together in this restaurant more than we could imagine. But this quick, we became too blind to see it wasn't us but God working this thing out. Our flesh rolled in like an erupted volcano at it's worst state. And I really had to admit, I was wrong and should had knew better because of the mistakes I've made before on jumping ahead of the Holy Spirit. And again, I was putting the Holy Spirit on the back burner and using my own instincts. We should had came to an understanding about each of our situations and the restaurant business, sat down and prayed to God to come up with a solution. Well the solution was already fixed for us, we were making money from all angles, thanks to the Lord but we just couldn't figure out what goes where. That's why we needed Prayer and obedience to God's answer.

But us two bull headed guys were like two head strong horses going in different directions. We said some words to each other and decided to separate the business. I was to take care of the caterans at the Firms and Ron was to take care of the restaurant. After being angry at each other the business wasn't the same. In God's word, Apostle Paul spoke about when we are angry, do not sin; do not let the sun go down on your wrath; Eph. 4:26. We stayed angry at each other day after day, therefore, we had moved into sin and God couldn't bless sin, we were fighting a losing battle. And I was thinking in my own selfishness that I had the upper hand now and will be able to pay my bills with no problem. At this time, to me paying my bills were the most important thing. All I had on my mind, was not to lose anything God had given me, which was still selfishness. We began on our separate quest with myself not realizing that his family were doing most of the cooking. So guess what, they refused to help me and now I was in the kitchen all by myself handling my own meals. I had to face them with unwelcome frowns but I was determined to accomplish what I started. I was a complete hard headed nut.

The gross from each job four times a week dropped from $500.00 dollars a day to $200.00 and sometimes $100.00 dollars a day. So the gross dropped considerably on the cateran and in the restaurant. We weren't only getting behind with our own bills but the restaurant was going under too. I was really struggling physically and mentally. My Van was having problems traveling so far everyday with no funds coming in, not even enough to get gas. I was having mechanical problems with my Van, whereas I couldn't afford to fix and problems were occurring inside the house also. It got so rough with things between my vehicle, the house, the cateran and with survival period. Everything just backfired and I almost couldn't take it, I even said to myself I did better when I was in the streets or the world. Then I said, at lease it didn't bother me as much when I had problems like this. Now it was really tormenting my mind because I knew being on this side, God was supposed to look out for you. I just couldn't understand why I was going through so much hell. I was praying every night and sometimes in the day and it seemed like God wasn't listening. I would even question God like Job did in the Bible. I was getting so down, one night I broke down in tears crying unto the Lord. I was crying so hard that the Holy Spirit came in the midst of my crying to remind me of what God brought me out of and brought me to. Through His love He gave me a new way of thinking and a new way of living. And most of all, He introduced Himself to me and took me to a whole new realm. Instead of crying for sadness, now I was crying for gladness, saying to myself, I will surely praise the Lord all the days of my life.

I came to myself and realized God couldn't bless a mess. Otherwords, I was still living in sin, by not forgiving my partner for the misunderstanding. I do thank God for everything because even in our own mess we create, God's grace and mercy steps in and stirs things up. One night I came in from a long frustrating day, prayed and prepared myself for bed. When I fell off to sleep, I had a dream about the situation Ron and I was going through and someone came into the dream and was pulling on me so much that I awakened. Every time I tried to go back to sleep he pulled on me worst than before. It was like I was fighting whatever it was pulling on me. I tossed and turned all night, like I was wrestling with someone. I got up to change rooms to avoid the interruptions because I had to get up early before the sun rose the next morning. The same was happening there, so I got up and went back to my bed hoping I could go back to sleep. It was like something I read one time before in the Bible in Genesis 32:24 when Jacob wrestled with an Angel of the Lord and the Angel told Jacob to let Him go, for the day breaks. But Jacob told the Angel I will not let You go until You bless me. Well, I was running from room to room trying to get away, unlike Jacob I was begging for Him to let me go, so I could get some sleep. After getting back into my bed, the same thing was happening and it got worst and I got so tensed, I had to sit up and pray to God. He spoke to me to go in the morning to apologize and ask for forgiveness. After I came to an agreement with the Lord, it was like a heavy weight was lifted. God gave me peace again and I slept the next few hours like a new born baby.

The next morning I got up with a smile on my face, feeling confident that everything were going to be all right now. When I got to the restaurant, my partner was coming in a whole new attitude also. I apologized and asked for forgiveness and explained to him what happened to me in the night. He also confessed and said his wife had a long talk with him about our situation and that someone had to change, if not both. So we started preparing the food together for the day and discussing the plans for us to get everything back into shape. Because we had gotten behind on all the bills, almost to foreclosure. But thanks be to God, He is always on time. We came back together working the cateran and the restaurant. The poolroom next door was opening on the weekend nights as a nightclub so we thought we shall be reaping the benefits off it also, by cooking for their customers. By doing this we were able to catch up on the bills at home and at the restaurant. God showed me divine favor with my Landlord. I had gotten behind so far on my lease payment but the Landlord was very understanding and worked with me on whatever I could come up with. I knew this was God's divine favor, even with my utility bills, God showed me favor. I seen this with my own eyes and couldn't nobody convince me, it wasn't God. Because, with the time I struggled, everything were supposed to had been cut off but God spoke to me on each occasion on what to do and I followed His instructions. That's why, I know that He's real and very much alive. And what helped me with this divine favor at this time was when Bishop T.D. Jakes spoke about not abusing God's divine favor. This helped me not to take it for granted when God gives you divine favor through people.

The guys who owned the poolroom next door were watching every move we were making. They were anticipating on us to fold so they could expand their business. We weren't just contending with our own situations but also our neighbor. Regardless, we kept going forward toward accomplishing our goals. We would continue reading and reminding ourselves of God's mighty power. I decided to go along with Ron's plan, in opening a bank account and putting everything in there. I believed he must had forgotten his own plan because I had to convince and push him to carry out with it. Then Ron reminded me of the woman he wanted to hire. He wanted to take her slow because he said, "she used to run with a rough bunch and she might be kind of slick". We came to an agreement to hire her. Now we had her and Ron's nephew and sometimes a few more of his kids helping us out. We continued doing exceedingly abundantly all we could do to move off ground level. We still had the franchise on our minds so we worked harder than ever, I didn't stop for nothing. My girlfriend or shall I say friendgirl at the time told me I was from one extreme to another. Yes she was right, after viewing my life it was evident that I was an extremist. When I'm for something I'm for it and when I'm not, I'm not. I'm full blast when I'm up and the same way when I 'm down. I'm really down for the count in everything I'm in.

Since this last separation with Ron and I, I struggled so hard because of God's wrath on this situation. It really made me realize I was trying to do everything without God's approval. Even though, God had sat me down in times before and made sure I was rooted in His Word for such times as this, I was still forgetting that it was God who brought me this far. It was times when I used to ask Him for divine guidance every single day I arose and all day long. But now, I wasn't going to church or following God's direction. Yes, I was praying for God to help me out of my dilemmas but I wasn't getting into His presence and asking Him to give me direction. And since this last incident, it awakened me so I prayed to God to be a lamp for my feet and a light for my path. And before I knew it, I was studying under King David's ministry. I started reading at the beginning of Psalms, reading a chapter a day. Sometimes I had to meditate on one chapter for a whole week.

Ron and I were more pleasant with each other now. We were more focused in on the restaurant and the catering. I was trying to do what my partner wanted me to do to keep cooperation, just like I said once before, I'm from one extreme to the next. I wanted to keep the tightest ship as possible, keeping up with spending, wastes and every coin. But evidently, Ron didn't want the ship kept that tight. So he suggested that we split again, this time on good terms. He said, I was getting in his way in the restaurant and he could handle the restaurant himself, if I could handle the cateran myself. He told me he would even get some of his family to help me. And as usual I agreed, but this time I called on my sister and daughter, who were unemployed.

In the meantime, the new girl, who was a friend of Ron was working herself easily around the restaurant. She was easing more and more into the kitchen each day. Ron and I were running kind of busy keeping everything going, he was handling one thing and I was handling another and then we would come down the middle and pay the bills. The new girl was still easing on in the kitchen, she was troubling the cooks so much that they were threatening to quit. One of them did and the other one tried to stand his grounds but she was to conniving and manipulative. I brought it up to Ron telling him, "something is not right about this girl". She was doing an excellent job though, all by herself. She was exactly what we were looking for so we finally allowed her to move on in the kitchen because the other cook couldn't take her anymore so he quit too. I really believed that she was also observing me and Ron's relationship in the business. Anyway, this time when we split up the business, I kept God with me and I was studying and praying regularly. Every step and meal I made, I prayed to God to anoint the meals. It wasn't as much revenue coming in, compared to when my partner and I were running the food together, because when we worked together we kept plenty of good food, lots of it. He would make sure I wouldn't run out of food. But still, through prayers God made sure I made just enough to make it on the restaurant bills and on the house bills. I was allowing the Holy Spirit to dictate my every move.

Meanwhile, my partner was struggling trying to run the restaurant. He called me for advice and suggestions on how to produce more business for the restaurant. I told him, the reason I was doing well and in so much peace was because of the Holy Spirit. I told him, "allow the Holy Spirit to dictate your moves, instead of yourself. Seemed like more and more I was finding out, he wasn't connected to the Holy Spirit. One big hindrance, that causes us to lose connection with the Holy Spirit was pride and stubbornness, in which both of us had. I have to admit, it was stirred up in me and he would get it stirred up in me much easier. His wife once told me right in his face, he improved her prayer life by keeping her on her knees because of his stubbornness and pride. Regardless, I got to my advertising skills to promote the business again, people were coming back in again and we got back in shape at the restaurant. We stayed out of each others way much as possible. But it seemed like, every time we came together in agreement with each other we prospered, it never failed. God really recognized us when we came together in agreement. People were coming in trying us out from everywhere.

By surprise, this certain young man and his wife came in to eat and to see what we had did with the place. He was the same young man who accepted Christ in his life back on my job. I had prophesied that one day he'll come back just to show me, he was walking in the Holy Spirit. And this was the day God brought it to pass. I was so happy for him and I thanked God right there on the scene. Not only that, but God also brought these guys by, who laughed and mocked at me on this same job. They mocked me when I told them how God was putting a vision in my spirit of started a business with only four hundred and fifty dollars. They came in to eat and was looking around with amazement. God has His time with everyone, it's a blessing seeing how God shows His wonderful works in our lives to let us know He is real and He does live in our lives.

Everything were working perfectly, the owners next door were watching us and I knew by statements, they wanted our restaurant and wanted us to fall by the wayside. Every time we had a spat or fight with each other, they were right there hoping we would close up and go our separate ways. They didn't know this thing was bigger than us because God was running things, even when we messed up. He would come and clean it up and put us back on track just in time. Like I said before, everything were going well and we were doing everything together and the new girl was working out as well. Our meals got better and better. We then hired another one of Ron's friends, one of his next door neighbors. So we had the head chef who, I am going to call Sharon and the prep lady who I am going to call Betty. Both were outstanding and were doing a fine job.

Ron and I were staying on the weekends, catching the business from the nightclub next door. We were collecting good money from them, but we had to face some hellish people, coming in intoxicated and rude. It started becoming a burden on the both of us, we wanted to get away from the wickedness but we needed the money. I do believe God will take from the wicked and give to

THE BOY IN THE MIDDLE

His people but we had to endure on this one. We tried to keep and exercised good standards and morals on a day to day basis. And we kept our integrity by going back to church on Sundays to keep some on time Word in us.

But still, as time went on in the club scene, it was getting the best of Ron and I. Otherwords, the club scene was rubbing off onto us, we were getting more and more in compromising with them in certain areas. I believed we were getting in the flesh more, no matter how hard we fought. Ron was much stronger in this area than I, maybe because he was married and had a family. Ladies were coming in half dressed, wearing all kinds of revealing clothes, flirting and giving jesters on how available they were. Drug pushers were coming in flashing their money around wanting to be treated special. And to be perfectly honest with you, unlike Ron, this was rougher on me than him, because it was stirring up old memories of when I was in the world and on this same scene. I felt myself comforming to their style again in talking and even sneaking drinks. Some people who knew me before came in thinking, since I had the restaurant, I was selling drugs again. I tried to shake them off jokingly but I didn't really make them think any differently. This was an act of pride and I knew it right then as I was talking to them, in which was enmity to God. I was headed for a fall and didn't realize it at the time. I guess my flesh had arose so much by the half dressed women and the slipping of alcohol drinks. And with the pride in me, God was allowing me to deceive myself.

One night I got off work from the restaurant and went next door to drink a beer. One thing led to another, I began to think about finding me a woman as I was coming back to Greenville toward home. I decided to stop in town at a few bars, trying to see what I could get into. This first occasion was one of a few and what led to these occasions were because of my own actions and weaknesses of the flesh. I became so vulnerable by teasing and rejecting so many women that was coming in the restaurant and on the catering. I was overwhelmed with so much flirting, it was a massive temptation while on the job but I withstood it until these few occasions. Anyway, I drunk a few beers at each bar and the funny thing about it was, just a few weeks ago I was in church at a drug abuse class pronouncing to a guy not to be afraid of the thought of drinking a beer. He was saying, he couldn't drink one beer without fearing he would start back drinking and doing everything else. I literally told this guy, the more he had Christ in him the less he had to fear drinking one beer. Otherwords, just because I was in a compromising state of mind, I was actually encouraging this guy to drink a beer, even though, he was a recovering alcoholic. I was thinking since you knew who you was in

Christ and rooted, you wouldn't have to fear going backwards because your mind was made up. But I didn't know the plans God had for this man and from this, God began opening my eyes to my stupid words.

So the first place I stopped in was a strip joint nightclub, where women were taking their clothes off, down to the G-string. When I first went in, the owner was behind the bar serving drinks and when I walked up to him, he gave me the rudest look I've ever seen and he wouldn't let up. I ordered a beer and he got worst and worst by talking trash to me for no reason at all. I couldn't understand what was going on because all I wanted was to drink a beer and look at a few girls. Even though, I was in the wrong place and had mischievous on my mind, God's anointing was still on me and the demons in him couldn't stand it at first sight. It was until I took a few drinks and was indulging in some of the activity, then he finally came around. At first I said to myself, I was just going to look but it seemed like the more I looked and drunk, the closer I wanted to get to the girls. And before the night was over, I ended up with a private dance in the back room and spending more than I attended to. Afterwards, I felt so ashamed and on my way home I had to repent to my God and I promised Him I will never let it happen again. But guess what, a month later I was going through it again. I found myself back at another strip nightclub in another one of my vulnerable moves. Each time this happened, I was going through a lonely state in my life and was desiring a woman. Anyway, I ended up in the backroom for another private dance. Before leaving the dancer, she said you must be a christian. It stunned me when she said this and I wondered how did she know. I left there again ashamed in the sight of God.

Yet again, this time about a few weeks later I found myself drinking beer again after closing the restaurant. Then I wanted to go somewhere to drink something stronger. So I went from nightclub to nightclub drinking shots of liquor and was desiring a woman more and more. I allowed myself to come under the familiar spirit of alcohol, in which it took total control of me. I came almost five minutes from home trying to satisfy my ego or my desire. I went straight back to town, I rode and rode and still couldn't find what I was looking for. I shouldn't been looking for anything but my mind was deceptive and God gave me every way to escape my condition but I didn't accept it. So God gave me over to a debase or reprobate mind, to those things which are not fitting; Romans 1:28. I finally stopped in this after hour spot, where young and old mixed, doing almost everything. I sat there and drank a couple of beers and mingled with a few old friends, who were still hanging out from when I was out there before. Nothing had changed except time and they were still sitting and hanging out, older and worn out.

But anyway, my debased mind was only for one thing and that was to find a woman to satisfy my need, which I thought I was so mostly due. A woman came toward me talking the right tune that I wanted to hear as if she was reading my mind. I knew in my heart God had saved me before, when I was in the streets. And I dared not push my Lord in taking a chance with myself like this. But I was in this debased mind and I said to myself, if I get some protection I'll be alright and I'll ask God for forgiveness. I thought this was something I was most desperately needing. The woman and I came to an agreement with the funds and all she wanted was some crack. So I gave her twenty dollars and she got her some crack and she got into the van. We rode until we found a spot to do what I wanted to do. When we got to that moment, she wanted to hit her some crack, so I allowed her to while I was getting undressed. The more she was getting into her drugs, the more my body and mind were changing. It was just like I had never been off drugs, immediately, I was craving for the drugs instead of sex. I started putting back on my clothes and she noticed so she asked me, "you want some of this crack don't you"? I told her, "I don't know what's going on with me because I've been off crack for four years". But I'm getting this urge in me like I've never quitted. I took a hit and my craving or joning was back. She said, "slow down we don't have much and this supposed to be for me". I assured her, we'll get some more, and that's what we ended up doing. Spending the money little by little, all that was in my pocket, we hit crack until daybreak.

I was so out of control, I didn't realize where I was until daybreak, which was Sunday morning. Even worst, we were only three houses down from the church I grew up in. I'm sure the Holy Spirit was reminding me of who I was and I felt bad and uncomfortable so I encouraged the girl to relocate, then we went around the corner. I was back where I left off, spending everything I had until I couldn't spend anymore, no matter how much. I made a couple of trips to the bank, where I was just able to save a little from the cateran. I withdrew all I could for that day, before I finally came to my senses. Finally, I told the woman that was enough, it's time I quit and go home. I realized then, I had messed up with myself and my Lord. I worried more about my God being upset with me than spending the money. I dropped the woman at her relatives house and she saw the disappointed expression on my face. She told me she was sorry she didn't get to satisfy my need. She even tried to have sympathy for me and told me, when I get myself back together, come by sometime and let her go to church with me. Then she asked me to pray for her to be delivered from drugs. See I had testified how God brought me out of this world and set my feet on solid ground. And how long I've been delivered from drugs until now. I told her, just because of my weakness for sex I ended up doing something I said I will never do again. On the way home I hated myself for failing to God and myself. I prayed all the way home and when I got home I fell on my face in repentance to God. I cried out to Him like a kid to his father, knowing what I did was wrong and real bad. I prayed to God to never allow me to go down that road again. And I prayed to God to put this day behind me as if it never happened. I went into a deep sleep, like a worn out baby who hadn't slept for days. The next morning, I awakened with full joy, God said joy cometh in the morning and by this I knew God hadn't took His love from me. I felt His love was with me still, as if nothing had happened. As of today, I haven't even thought of crack, not even an urge or craving. God wiped it away in one day as well forgotten. Might of fact, I'm as against it now than I've ever been before.

Oh yeah, one thing I just couldn't get out of my mind was the fact that I told that fellow in church, don't be afraid of the one beer he couldn't drink. God showed me right here, no matter how much you are in God, you still can't play with fire or you will soon or later get burnt. I prayed hard to God to not allow that guy in church to be misled by my ignorance. And the reason I'm telling all my business is because I want you to beware of all the things on your journey with God. I believed one big reason I went through these fatal experiences were because I didn't have a per-say spiritual father to really listen to right here on earth. Another reason could have been, when I came from the otherside or streets to this side in the kingdom, I was a free-styler, otherwords, It was to hard to sat under authority. So the Holy Spirit took me under His wing and taught me the hard way on everything. And I have to say, I thank God, He did. I also thank Him for never leaving me nor forsaking me.

THE RIDE GETS TOUGHER

In the restaurant, everybody were working together according to plans, it was like clockwork. Business were flowing good, the catering was moving right along and one of the Firms gave us an extra day. One day was a meat and three, the other was a fast food day. God kept on being faithful to us as if He was showing us and everybody else, what He does for His children. God was blessing us so much, I noticed when we carried the meals to the Firms, God stretched the food. I told Ron after a successful run, I believed God did something in the meal, because I had added up to the highest projection on what to expect but we made more. And not only that, we were supposed to had ran out a long time ago. After we counted up it was double than what I had projected. I told Ron, "we have to praise Him in this", He was showing us miracle after miracle, letting us know face to face His power. Right here, He(God) was showing us His mighty power from the scripture; Matthew 14:17, when He fed the five thousand people with only five loaves of bread and two fish.

Brothers and sisters, when you are not sure you can make it on this otherside, just believe God with all your mind, with all your heart and soul and nonetheless, all your might, He(God) will show you a way to survive. Even with all the hustlers, who hesitate about coming on the Lord's side because of sacrificing your so-called skills with money. God will make a way for you to survive and see His promise and your dreams come to actions. I'm praying that all will come and see for yourselves the good taste of the Lord in your mouth and the fullness down in your belly. I'm not sayings you won't go through, during all my adversities and sufferings, I really learned how to trust the Lord. "I mean really trust Him", we say with our mouths, we trust the Lord and love Him but when the test and trials come, then we really have to prove what the mouth is saying. The Holy Spirit brought this scripture to my attention during my trials in Psalms 37:5, which states; Commit your way to the Lord, trust also in Him and He shall bring it to pass. This scripture was an on time scripture for me at this particular time, but what really captured my attention was the way King David put it. Reading about King David's situations and conditions that he went through made me wonder why he said, "trust also in the Lord". The "also" is what stunned me, because it was like he was adding something else in this scripture. So while I was in my situations and going through my conditions I sought the Holy Spirit for help. While sitting in Bible study one night, I was listening to the church recite the same scripture I had asked the Holy Spirit to reveal to me. I was brought to a lowly place in my spirit with a contrite spirit also, after reading this scripture it became so real to me from all the pain and suffering I had to endure that taught me to really trust God, it wasn't any lip service anymore. One trust I had to develop most dearly was trusting God to give me a paycheck from the restaurant every week. It wasn't like a job, when you know what you are getting every week. So I couldn't budget because I didn't know from week to week what I might receive. I just followed God's instructions on what to do with my bills and I have to tell you He was there.

In the restaurant it was always something going on and if I talked about everything that went on, I would be writing forever. But the Holy Spirit had me writing to glorify the Lord's name. I personally had to get back focused because of the incident with the girl and the drugs in the last chapter. I had to keep myself from participating with the nightclub next door. The owners went as far as trying to merge with us to get liquor license. See in the state of South Carolina, before a nightclub can sell liquor they have to have a grill to be able to cook. And since we were joined together, they wanted us to sub-lease the building to them in order to sell liquor. First we just plainly rejected them, but they kept insisting, then we had to let them know it was against our morals because it wasn't godly. But they kept on insisting anyhow to the point where they were offering deals in order for us to bend our standards. We were participating in their business too much already. We definitely knew if we went further it would've been over for us. And furthermore, the owner of this nightclub next door was a Deacon in church but he was greedy for gain at any means necessary. The good thing God was doing for me at this particular time was being a lamp for my feet and a light for my path by having me reading from Psalms during King David's ministry. And at this particular time God gave me something to really meditate on from Psalms 50:16-23, which states;

> But to the wicked God says; what right have you to declare My statues, or take my covenant in your mouth, seeing you hate instructions and cast My words behind you? when you saw a thief, you consented with him, And have been partakers with adulterers.

You give your mouth to evil, and your tongue frames deceit. You sit and speak against your brother; You slander your own mother's son. These things you have done, and I kept silent; You thought, I(God) was altogether like you; But I will rebuke you, And set them in order before your eyes. Now consider this, you who forget God, Lest I tear you in pieces, and there be none to deliver: Whoever offer Praise glorifies Me(God); And to him who orders his conduct alright I will show the salvation of the Lord.

When I read this chapter, I immediately felt like God was talking to me and Ron and the guys next door in the poolroom. So I showed the chapter to Ron and explained to him what the Holy Spirit revealed to me. Then we came to the conclusion of not cohering with them in any crooked way.

We were continuing taking care of business together and everything were going well. Once again we were getting ahead slowly but surely. We were trying to stay focused on the business and God's rhema Word. We came together to meditate and praise God on how beautiful He was. Little that we knew, satan was creeping up on us, it seemed like every time we came together to do what was right, satan was right there on our track trying to come between us. The guys next door were watching our every move, since we wouldn't honor their request. I told Ron, I wouldn't be surprised if they were wishing we would fall to the wayside so they could come in and claim everything, but thanks be to God and His keeping power.

The head cook had moved in pretty deep now. She was running just about everything in the restaurant, even the business next door. Ron and I were trusting her more and more, we were depending on her more and by doing this, we quickly ran into a big mistake. She was turning more into insubordination, not only trying to take over the kitchen but also trying to tell Ron and I what to do and when and where to do it. I came in daily to check out everything to make sure things were alright and fresh. She would literally demand me out and warn me not to come back in the kitchen. Each day got more and more tensed. At first, I thought she was just thankful for her job and wanted us to feel assured, she had it. But everyday got worst, a controlling spirit had taken her over. She was ordering Ron and I around and on top of that she had problems accepting changes we were making to benefit the company. If it wasn't coming from her it wasn't a good idea. She had gotten very harsh and demanding toward the other help also. Then she started getting manipulative to Ron and I, probably from when we were going through the separations, she was learning our personalities, our strengths and most of all our weaknesses.

Anyway, she started manipulating Ron against me and was very effective with it. He came to me one day out of the clear blue and told me I needed to stay on the caterans more and leave the restaurant business to him, he could handle everybody there. So, that's what I did, I left him in charge to keep the peace. But I had to tell him this before I left, with us being partners to the point of marriage to each other in this business, we can't afford to let an outsider come in and turn us against each other. Nevertheless, I went on my way to continue to handle my business with the cateran. Whenever I came back to the restaurant to regroup she would frown up at me and talk harshly, like I didn't mean anything to her. And Ron wouldn't say a word, which made me feel like I was a stranger in my own restaurant but I just kept coming and going, taking care of business as usual. Finally, I really got fed up with the sarcastic remarks from her and asked Ron to do something about it. I guess he did because now I was getting the quiet treatment and the mumbling of words under her breath. I had to tell her one day about her attitude and remind her that I was paying their wages and taking care of the restaurant bills too. Then after telling her this, she would come to me real humble and conning with an unbelievable change, feeding my mind with negativity things about Ron and what he does when I'm not around. Then I would say some unnecessary things about Ron, she was bringing a bone and carrying bone, right under our nose before we realized it.

Ron and I gained more hostility toward each other until our spirits were separated again. Now here we were going down this road again, swinging bats at each other, sort of speaking. When we came in we wouldn't speak to each other, I would do my preparing for the cateran and he would do his preparing for the restaurant without saying a word to each other unless just for business. Our anger grew toward each other more and more. Through our flesh we were allowing satan to have his way with us. We were so blind and couldn't see that satan was trying to keep us separated, divided we fall. To keep God's saints from prospering in the Spirit and in the natural, satan loves to keep us separated from each other. Now I was contending with my partner and the head cook too. She got worst and worst toward me, talking boldly against everything I was doing. Ron was right there on her side as if she was his partner, they had became such a team with each other.

They were over charging and cheating people out of their money, I questioned Ron and he okayed what she was doing. After seeing this crookedness, it burdened me and loaded me down with oppression. I had been trying to be very fair financially and now after seeing this I wondered now could they be trusted. I went to my friendgirl house under such distress from this tension, hoping I could release my burden to someone before I explode. I explained to her my situation and how I was trying to play fair and didn't want them to bring out the old me. I told her before God changed me I was the worst of the worst in cheating, conniving and conning people. And I didn't want to bring this side of me back to keep up with them. It hurt me so bad, I broke down in tears, crying on her shoulder unto the Lord. She sat me down and gave me a word of wisdom and sent me on my way. Everyday I came to work I felt the hostility coming from them, it got so bad with us, the oppression in me grew stronger. But God did have one of the cooks with a heart of gold. She helped me anyway she could, even though they told her not to. I became so angry with them, something like a silent angry. Otherwords, when they raised hell, I raised hell back or otherwise I wouldn't say a word.

When I went to church all my praise and joy were gone, I couldn't even shout hallelujah anymore. Week after week it was the same thing, sitting in church in despair. I had lost my joy from my problems that caused me to live in the flesh. I really didn't want to go to church but for somehow or some reason I was hoping going would change things. I felt like I was in this world all alone, that no one understood where I was. And if I tried to explain they still wouldn't understand. One night, when coming home from the restaurant I stopped at the old church I used to go to and I caught them in the middle of their Bible study. So I sat down and listened to their service. By listening to their teachings and questions, a door was opened for me to explain the situation between the head cook and me. I told them, it was like a demon was assigned to me right under my nose to irritate me all day long. I told them, I tried to rebuke her openly and she wasn't moved, surprisely, she turned and rebuked me back. I knew then, I was under no power from God. Two of the saints told me I was feeding satan as long as I was fighting him in the flesh. They told me to quit mouth battling with her and get back in the Spirit. The next morning, I awakened with joy, feeling that it was a new day and sure enough it was. The power of the enemy was to no effect because I didn't feed into it. Instead I kept my mind on Jesus Christ and how great He is. I thanked God for those two saints at the church, who rescued me with the Word of God. So now she was to no effect on me.

But I still had Ron to contend with, and not only were our relationship stale but the business was sinking also. God took His blessings off it every time we got into these divisions. We should had known better by now and realized this wasn't good for us but we were wrapped up in our own opinions, instead of checking with God's opinion. The cateran business slowed down because of the lack of help I was getting. But God was allowing me again to just make it. The restaurant wasn't doing too good neither, just enough to turn money right back in it but not enough to pay any bills. Ron was under frustration because of what was going on, to the point of blaming me for the conditions. I was trying to keep myself fine tuned to the Lord because I didn't want a repeat like before. Plus, I was reading in the book of Psalms at the time and it was helping me keep my composure by reading about King David in his distress. Furthermore, during this time I dreamed a strange dream that I owned a pet white snake. Everyday when I opened the cage to feed him, he raised his head in a striking position each time. I never payed any attention to it though, I thought it was just the snake's personality. I kept this snake for years and it raised up in the striking position each time I tried to feed it. Finally, the snake was out growing me so I decided to give it to the zoo. So I packed the white snake up and took it down to the zoo. When I got there I looked around the zoo for a little while until the zoo keeper came out to see what I had to give them. The zoo keeper looked at the snake and took it to his Lab for research. He came out and asked me, "how long have you had this snake"? I told him, I had him for some years now, he looked at me stunned. Then he asked me, do you know you've been housing one of the most dangerous snakes in the world? He also asked me, "how did you keep from getting bit by it"? I told him, I didn't do anything. He said, one bite from this snake would have killed you instantly, I smiled and left. The next morning, when I awakened from the dream it didn't phase me at the time. But the more I thought about it, I started questioning myself and God. I didn't get an answer right away so I went on about my business as usual, not thinking about it anymore.

Then in Sunday school, the teacher mentioned snakes in the class. He talked about snakes in reference of curses, when I heard this I was reminded of the dream so I said okay Lord what is going on with this snake. I still couldn't grasp what was going on at this time. I kept asking the Lord for revelation and when you ask God for revelation He will give it to you. I couldn't see it at first, then the Holy Spirit made it clearer and clearer to me. The Holy Spirit revealed to me that the white snake in the house was someone close to me that was praying against me. And with the snake being white, it meant they were wolves dressed in sheep clothing. They were portraying righteousness but they were praying evil things. Then the Holy Spirit reminded me of my partner, when he prayed against this guy he owed money to. He prayed that God get rid of this guy and the guy died the next day. He also had told me he prayed against his uncle and aunt once and the aunt got bad off sick. On top of this, Ron had just recently prayed against another one of his uncles because he kept bothering Ron about the money he owed him from a job he done for Ron. Ron had told me his uncle was going to die in two weeks. I immediately rebuked Ron for saying that by telling him, that was witchcraft he was using. I told him it wasn't Christlike to pray evil on someone. So the Holy Spirit brought all this back into remembrance to me. Then I thought to myself, if Ron prayed against his own family, how much more will he pray against me.

I approached him with my dream and then with the answer I received from the dream. He was stunned when I told him and he gave me a gritty smile. I really got to my praying time, night and day for protection. And God did hear my prayers because He put me back into a deep sleep and gave me another dream, this time a dream of hope. I dreamed, I was at this lake with some professional fishermen trying to make a catch. I knew I was out gunned because they had their professional clothing and gear on. I just wanted to make a catch for myself to go home and eat. All of a sudden I had a bite, I started reeling it in and I was having a hard time doing it. Finally, I got the fish up in the air and while reeling the fish in, it was so big, the fish had baby fish jumping out and back into his mouth. All the professional fishermen dropped their rods and ran down to see this amazing catch. They sat there looking with their mouth wide open, saying, not only is it the biggest fish they've seen but it has small fish jumping up out of it's mouth. They congratulated me for such a successful catch.

I awakened from my sleep with this dream heavily on my mind, wondering what did it mean. I knew the dream was from God because of the last dream so I started trying to put things together myself, instead of asking or waiting on God. I came to a conclusion that God was going to grant me a restaurant of my own close to home with everything already furnished. I went out looking for restaurants that had went out of business. And I found a few of them already furnished and I said to myself time after time, this is it. I didn't tell Ron what I was doing because I wanted it to be a surprise. I wanted to separate so bad that I went and called one of my hustling buddies for financial help. But that wasn't it neither, God wasn't intending on anything like that happening, especially when I was running in the flesh instead of the Spirit. I constantly allowed my flesh to take over my spirit and that wasn't good. Like I said before, God won't bless a mess. I finally settled down and decided to let God handle what ever this hope was He stirred up in me. By letting God handle the situation, now I had a peace in me with hope and faith.

Ron and I were still in a separated spirit and we were still showing stubbornness toward each other, neither one wanted to submit first. I said to myself, I am always the one who submit first and when I submits first that makes Ron think he's always right and I'm always wrong. Because of the separation between the two, it wasn't too pleasant for me around the restaurant. It was still more people against me than for me, even the families were coming in looking at me strange. So when I came in, I just cooked my food for the catering and it had got to the point where I could hardly do that. The head cook started complaining again, this time it was about me being in the way when I prepared for the catering. No matter how I rearranged my time and position, it still wasn't good enough. But I didn't feed into it because I had to keep my concentration. The agony got so bad again, I had to ask her to be dismissed until further notice. She was surprised and immediately went to Ron to be rescued. He came to me and I told him this was standing for now.

We continued without her and was doing good, even though, she came back continuously asking for her job back. She humbled herself to me until she started crying for her job back. I finally gave in but under certain conditions and she agreed. The first week she came back she was quiet and nice. On one of my caterings, I had to prepare a very expensive and important meal. I came in the night before to prepare it and I had great success once I finished. People had been asking for this dish for a long time so I cooked a double portion. And when I got there with the dish, people jumped on it like it was going out of style. I was making good money on the dish until some of the people came back telling me something was wrong with the dish. They said, It tasted like vinegar was in it. My servers and I investigated it and sure enough it had been spiked. When I got back to the restaurant, the head cook was the first person questioning me about the dish. Then she asked could she tastes it and she asked did we do good with it. Right then, I knew for certain she had spiked the dish but I wouldn't give her the gratification to talk negative about it. Instead, I was very much positive and thankful to God for the returns we made off it. And I knew God had stepped in to help me from losing everything. I kept it to myself for a while because of the conditions with Ron and I.

One day, the ice was broken from our spirits being separated in the most unusual way. And it wasn't a time too soon because we were sinking in the restaurant bills again. The guys in the bar next door knew we were sinking and they were planning on us to give up and hand the restaurant over to them. Their desires and wishes were for us to fold but thanks be to God once more for watching over us. He took me to chapter 140 of Psalms and put my mind on what was happening with us and the guys next door. Psalms 140 talked about the wicked setting traps and schemes on you and desiring you to stumble. I surely believed when we broke the ice, it was a set up from God. This is what happened, we came in the restaurant one day expressing our opinion toward each other and we laid everything on the table and the more we expressed ourselves the more vehemently and intensed our conversation got. It was to the point, we said we hated one another and we said, we hated we ever met. I had to go out to get grocery for the catering and the restaurant, so I left. While going down the road I was really upset so I put in a cassette by Apostle William L. Bonner to get my mind off the situation. Apostle William L. Bonner was a great influence in my life at this particular time and still is as of this day. God had me put this particular tape in at this particular time. Apostle Bonner was preaching about our wars and battles are not carnal but powerful through the blood of Jesus Christ. He said, God has put a weapon in our hand and the weapon is the Blood. He said, anytime the devil comes against us, we have the Blood of Jesus Christ to use against him. After hearing this intense message, I told God when I get back to the restaurant I'm going to sprinkle oil all over the doors because satan had to leave that place. I had got so intensed off this message, I couldn't hold it any longer. While driving down the road I was pleading the Blood and rebuking the enemy myself. When I reached the restaurant, I had made plans to plead the Blood and sprinkle oil everywhere but when I opened the door the dark cloud in there had cleared up, it looked like a new light was in the place. Ron had a big smile on his face and when I seen this I said, hallelujah. I told Ron, "I was getting ready to run that devil out of here through the Blood of Jesus". But it looked like God had beat me there, hallelujah. So we apologized to each other and made our amends to each other. He told me God had started dealing with him while I was gone.

We realized that we had work to do and we had to get busy getting the restaurant back in shape. We were about broke again but we were willing to move forward with what God gave us. Things were coming together slowly. On one of my meditation days, I was reading in Psalms chapter 34 and this chapter caught my attention. It was saying how God delivered King David out of all his troubles and from all his fears. I went over it again and again, then I prayed to God to deliver us from all our troubles and fears. I even brought this chapter up to Ron and we sat down and read it over together. I told him God was trying to tell us something through this chapter but we still couldn't see or feel the deliverance coming from nowhere. We were months behind on bills because of the controversies we kept carrying ourselves through. I asked the Holy Spirit why can't we be delivered from this mess we were in. Then the Holy Spirit took me to the beginning of the chapter and had me read it again until I got a revelation. I had been missing the whole concept of what the chapter was saying. Before God can deliver you from all your troubles you need to bless the Lord at all times. His praise shall be continually in your mouth. My soul shall make it's boast in the Lord. Last but not least, David said, I sought the Lord, I wasn't seeking the Lord deep enough in my heart. I mentioned to Ron how the Holy Spirit made everything clear to me. So I went back to the Lord and got into my studies and fellowshipping with Him even harder. And I cried out to Him and repented for being slack in my worship and other things.

One day when I was coming back from one of my catering runs, the head cook asked did we need any money and jokingly I said yes. She was talking to her boyfriend on the phone, who happened to be a business man. She told me, he asked how much did I need and I told him again jokingly, five thousand dollars. She asked, when did you need it, then I stood to attention, noticing this guy sounded serious. I got on the phone to talk with this guy, I never met. I gave him a time to get back with him until I talk with my partner. Ron came in and I explained the situation and offer we just got and he was totally against it for a number of reasons, which I fully understood. I reminded him of the chapter I read about God delivering us out of all our troubles. We were so behind on everything that we needed the money right away to keep from being put out. I prayed and fasted to God for Ron and I on this situation. In the next two days Ron came in the restaurant in a whole new attitude. He told me, he thought it over and decided to go for it. To make a long story short, we got the money and started setting up for plans. And I saw it with my own eyes, when God said, He'll take your enemies and make them your footstool. He actually turned the hearts of my adversaries to help me and bless me when I needed it most.

We came up with a whole new menu just for everyday specials, hoping it would draw more customers. Then we made flyers and issued them throughout the neighborhoods. We advertised on the radio and caught up all our bills, it was a beautiful thing and everybody were happy. Money were coming in again day by day. We were all getting along and taking care of business together. We were partaking in the restaurant and the catering together. I would come in the middle of the day, more toward the end, starting my habits again checking on everything to make sure the food were fresh and things were clean and that everybody were getting charged properly. The head cook started to complain again about me checking on them. So Ron pulled me to the side and told me, he didn't mean any harm but he had the restaurant business now. Otherwords, he was saying, I needed to tend to the catering only. It stunned me at first but I remembered before, whenever Ron makes money he gets conceited, so I left him with one thing to remember. I told him, "before I let someone else sink this ship, I rather it be you and I". I left the restaurant in their hands once again and started concentrating on the cateran and paying my bills and half of the restaurant's bills.

Things were slowing down for me again but God still enabled me to make it. Then one day Ron called me complaining about how slow it had got and how he barely had enough to do anything with. He wanted me to pay all the help even though they weren't helping me. So once again, I came down to bail him out. The next few days we had a meeting and he wanted me to tell the help, we had to lay them off until further notice. Then Ron suggested that we close the restaurant to the public and just work the caterings. I couldn't help for reminding him of the statement I made about the sinking ship. He agreed to his mistake in relying on the head cook running things. Now, I decided to tell him how she tried to destroy one of my caterans by spiking one of my main entrees. He was really distraught with her.

We tried to run the caterings through the restaurant. He came in every morning to assist me and went back home and got in the bed. He did this everyday until he landed a second shift job and suggested that I get one too. In which wasn't a bad idea, except I wanted to keep things running in the business, so badly. I thought about what Bishop T.D. Jakes said, about how black businesses don't make it a full year and we were about a month from a year. I seen more and more that he was giving up so I offered to buy him out so I could move on with the business but he refused. He Probably thought that I would had got things going in his own home town. I continued doing my best by myself, trying to keep things going. I'd got to the point, where I wanted the restaurant opened again, so I tried to run the restaurant and the catering with the little help I had. Ron saw what I was trying to do so he came to me and told me he didn't want anything to do with the restaurant anymore. He wanted to get completely out, I guess this meant that he wanted us to close it down. Because he didn't want me to buy him out and he was kind of hesitate on selling, fearing we wouldn't get enough.

One day after a very tiring catering run, I was very disgusted of everything. Trying to pay everything everywhere, it seemed like everything were going wrong. I was feeling like giving up myself at this time. When I came in the restaurant to unload everything, there was a guy who had took over the nightclub next door from the other guys, coming in behind me. He looked around and asked me, was I interested in selling the place. It was the right timing for the offer, my soul lit up inside with enjoyment but I couldn't let him see it. He gave me an offer and I gave him one back and we came to an agreement. Now I had to bring this offer to Ron, knowing in my heart he would be excited. Sure enough, when I told Ron he was excited like me. Even now, God knew our despair and instead of allowing us to lose completely or all together. He provided a Ram in the bush for us, as He did for Abraham. God is so wonderful,so great, so loving that we have to praise Him with our last breath.

We made the deal and cleaned out everything they didn't buy. Ron didn't want anything so I ended up with all the extras, which were pretty good to me. Now I could see what God was showing me in the dream of the big fish with the little fish coming out it's mouth. The Chicken Of The Sea Restaurant was over now. We were able to pay off our debtors and still had money left over. Ron was kind of looking sad, standing with his wife so I gave Ron a final word before we departed. I told him, "you don't have to look disappointed about anything because we tried something a lot of people wouldn't have tried, especially with the amount of money we had to start with". God blessed the restaurant and if we hadn't been negligent, it would be still going strong. I told Ron, I call ourselves "Mountain Climbers" because we'll always be trying to climb another mountain somewhere.

THE TRANSFORMATION

After receiving everything from the restaurant, I was still refusing to give up. I continued to work the catering from my home. I bought some other necessary equipment to continue processing the dinners for the Firms. Now it was only me and my sister working it out. I desperately searched high and low for another restaurant closer to home. Hoping I could do a whole lot better with my own family. My sister and I kept running the business, trying to keep the news about the restaurant concealed. We both were making enough money to pay our bills, but I was living a hypocritical lie and didn't realize it. God was trying to pull me back into His presence, but my mind had became all into myself. I really thought I could do this thing all by myself, it was all about me now. This was the time I really needed God but I was too stupid to realize it.

Even though, I was staying away from women so that I wouldn't sin, I was still teasing them while on the cateran job and calling different ones every other night and not really letting them know I was God's child. I thought, as long as I didn't take it any further, I was alright. I had became the biggest fool, taking on everything in my own hands. That's why Jesus spoke in John 15:5 when He said, I am the vine, you are the branches. He who abides in Me and I in him, bears much fruit; for without me you can do nothing. I had to learn this the hard way as everything else. I was having a whole lot of fun on the caterans until one of the most influential Firms dropped all their vendors from coming to their place. I was getting my highest revenue from this place and now it was cut right out from under my feet, it was a big blow for my pockets. Then one of the other Firms had a major lay-off and laid off over three to four hundred people, and this was another major blow. Now my sister and I were generating with just one leg but I was still refusing to give up and I was still trying to keep hope alive. I went around to other Firms just like Ron and I did when God blessed us at first, hoping I could have this blessing again. I represented my portfolio, calling myself stepping out on faith but I was perpetrating a lie. Because I was still trying to operate under the CHICKEN OF THE SEA restaurant, when it no longer existed.

I had gotten so beside myself, I was in total ignorance of what I was doing. I was blinded by my own ego.

After going to these different Firms, I could see how desperately I needed another restaurant. I really hit the pavement then, searching and thinking this would save the business. I even had my sister and mother involved in my quest for survival. My mother was trying to tell me to check with God on which direction to take. But I totally ignored her, thinking it wasn't anybody closer to God like I was. I thought, if God was trying to pull me in another direction, I would surely know. I saw one of the DEHEC health inspectors out one day and we sat down and talked. I told him what happened to the restaurant and then I told him what I was trying to do. He explained to me very carefully to beware of people with buildings of out dated codes. He said, they will take your money and not tell of the situation of the building. I thanked him for that information but had soon forgotten what he told me because of my anxiety. God had placed this man in my path so that I wouldn't make any further mistakes.

My sister and I were continuing working just two days a week, it had jumped from four good days to two hope we make it days. One out of these two Firms were getting word about the closing of the restaurant. So now, this was causing more anxiety to build up in me to take the first building I saw open. And that's just what I did, I seen a cute little building with a restaurant set-up in it, I went straight ahead, fully charged, forcing action so I could save the business. My mother tried to warn me again but I was bullheaded and looking at one thing. Guess what! I paid the owner of the building my last dime. When I went to get the permit for the building, they told me this building had been re-zoned and could not be used for a restaurant, period. On top of this, they said the owner knew about this already. So I went back to the owner not knowing he was going to refuse to give me back my money. Right now today, I have a civil suit on him for this money. I lost my money and one of the other two accounts I had. So now, my sister and I had only one account to go to, which wasn't even worth the time. I told my sister, "lets pack it up, I guess it's over".

My mom told me to try to get a job and maybe God will allow me to get a restaurant again one day. I was still agitated about the situation and deep in my soul I didn't want to give up this easy. I went on a three day fast with nothing to eat, to try to get back in tuned with God, for His divine direction. My bills had started getting behind again, so now I was humbling myself to listen to my mother. Why do we have to be dead empty, before we listen to someone? Or why does it take point zero to be able to humble ourselves?

Anyway, on my second day of fasting, I went to the supermarket to get some items. When I came back to my van, I took my keys to open the back and I placed my items in the back. Then I walked to the driver side and put my keys in to unlock the door. When the door unlocked, I reached for the door handle to open the door and the door automatically locked back before I could open it. I put my keys in it again and it done the same thing before I was able to open the door. I said to myself, what in the world is going on. I tried it again and it repeated itself again, so I went to the passenger side and the same thing happened to it. I then, went to the back remembering I had gotten in it earlier. It was locked also and was doing the same as the other doors. Right then, I had to pause, because this had never happened before. I thought about the "fast" I was on and right away, I knew the enemy(satan) was doing a supernatural thing here. I immediately said a prayer and rebuked the devil in the name of Jesus. I tried unlocking it again on the passenger side and the locks tried locking itself again but it was on a slower frequency. I was able to get in and as of this day, it hasn't happened again. I realized from this incident that satan was attacking me on this fast because he(satan) knew I was about to get back in tuned with God. And by this, I knew I was on the right track. I prayed to God that night and repented for my sins and for living in my flesh. This was becoming a regular thing for me, praying and repenting. Look like I should have learned by now.

The next day, I got up and went out looking for a job, I searched high and low and nothing occurred. Anyway, I started out again one early day, headed toward this temporary place, when all of a sudden God turned my whole direction to another temporary place I hadn't dealt with in a while. I went over to this temp place and as soon as I got in the door and sat down good, they remembered me and told me this was my lucky day. They told me a job just came open for two weeks and it's on first shift, I secretly, praised the Lord because this job was right on time, a life saver. Everything were behind now, so I felt like a refugee who just got rescued, I was so happy inside, nobody could imagine how much. I knew a couple of ministers, who told me, I was going backwards by leaving the restaurant business for a job. Even though, it was a step down, but between me and God, I really appreciated what He did for me. Otherwords, this was a special blessing to really know I would be getting a payroll check every week as long as I show up to work. See, a lot of people don't realize, when you own your own business, sometimes you don't get paid all the time. And this is what really caused me to trust God. But now I felt a relief and I knew I had to get my act together with God because God is faithful and will always be. He's faithful to us even when we're not faithful to ourselves or to Him.

I remembered when I was on the cateran, the Holy Spirit was telling me I needed to get back into Apostle Paul's ministry in the New Testament. But I was too busy at the time teasing the women to even take the Holy Spirit serious. The Holy Spirit was pushing me to study but I was pulling away. Right at this time of transition between occupations, I had a misunderstanding with my friendgirl that caused us to never communicate with each other again. So I got hysterical of the disconnection and prayed to God to send me a girlfriend that's similar to me. Oohh! what did I do that for because I was already a mess by myself. The next day, I met this lady and this relationship became more than I could handle. That's why I say, I believe I was pulling away faster than God was pushing me.

I came on this new job looking it over, not knowing if I would be here long. One of the guys kept asking me questions about myself and one of the questions were, where did you work last? I told him I just came from running my own restaurant,in which was one of the biggest mistakes I made. Every day he asked me more and more about the restaurant as if he didn't believe me. As time went by, he made jokes about me running the restaurant to comparing me to the job I was running now. The more he got to know me the more he tried to degrade me. This guy here, I'm talking about was my leadsman and supposedly had the responsibilities of a Supervisor.Finally, I had gotten myself to reading in Apostle Paul's ministry in the New Testament and it was coming right on time because it became more guys like him trying to degrade me and I became angry and prideful. I felt like I had to prove myself to them to keep my integrity. I stood many times trying to argue the point with these guys.

I remembered one day, I jumped on the forklift moving some material around and a leadsman from another department came through looking for some product. I was already pumped up by these guys, feeling like I had to prove my intelligence. I was boasting and bragging on how I was taking over in there. I started running my mouth to this leadsman for no reason at all. I jumped off the forklift with the forklift set in stable conditions. When all of a sudden, the forklift took off backwards in full speed as if someone put it in gear. The forklift crashed into some pallets five feet from us. If anybody, including myself would have been behind that forklift, would have got killed. It scared everybody because it hadn't did that before. I reported it to the Supervisor and he had a serviceman check it out and he said, it wasn't anything wrong with it. And as of this day it hadn't done it again. Later on, the Holy Spirit spoke to me, telling me He was trying to get my attention and the Holy Spirit added to my spirit, the bragging and boasting had to stop and

I needed to calm down. When God showed me how quick He could take my life, I knew then, I needed to get back into fellowship with Him. This thing that happened with the forklift was a supernatural act from God.

The biggest part of this adversity coming from the other guys were mainly because when I first got there God had gifted me with a sense of organizing. The place was in a mess so I started rearranging things they said could never happen and will never happen. And to have this done God blessed me with a partner who worked along side by side to help put it together. He was new also and agreeable with me in changing things around. And the good thing about this was that the head people in staff and our Supervisor loved the change. They had our back as long as we didn't get out of character and thanks to the Holy Spirit for helping me keep my composure. These guys who said it couldn't happen, seen it unfold right before their eyes and this made them really hate me even worst.

Months went by and I finally I got off temporary and went to permanent. At this time, I was still trying to get my mind back from living a carnal life. I was trying to allow my flesh to die so I could walk in the Spirit and contending with these guys on the job were like a uphill struggle. I was really struggling but the Holy Spirit was there helping me by telling me what I had to get rid of. One of the biggest problems I was wrestling with was me sleeping with my new girlfriend, that was the biggest no-no. And I knew it but I had started back compromising and justifying my actions in this relationship. See, she had told me she was Saved and in God too, when we met. But I never told her how much I loved Him and how I did desire His presence. So I tried letting her know what I had to do, because deep in my heart I was desiring God's fellowship again. I knew I had never shown her this part of me so she took it for a joke. Then she started rationalizing by saying, fornication was just a regular sin like every other sin we do day by day. She was saying, once Saved always Saved and God knows our weaknesses and know we desire to be loved by one another. So I went with what she was saying for a while until the further I got in Apostle Paul's ministry for God, the more my heart was getting more convicted.

Now I knew why I couldn't handle a lot of criticism from the guys at work, because I was still living in the flesh with my girlfriend. No matter how hard I was trying to get in the Spirit, the flesh was taking over. Now I was catching it from both ends. Otherwords, my girlfriend was getting upset with me now because I kept changing, going back and forth. I tried to do right at one time but when my lustful flesh aroused, I would yield to it. It was the same at work, I couldn't walk in the Spirit because I would turn right around and walk in the flesh. My flesh would have me talking about stuff my spirit wouldn't allow, like I said before I was in a struggle. One thing that really helped me out though, was the fact that I had asked God to be a lamp for my feet and a light for my path. Every time I was reading in the scriptures, it was coming to life. Otherwords, God was warning me of something coming in my path the very next day. It was coming so rapidly, I would miss it for myself, even though, I'd just read it. I had to ask God for forgiveness for missing it and to give me another chance to do what He had shown me to do. I had to pray to God now to help me recognize it right away and respond correctly as His word says.

One of the guys who had a better job than I kept coming in my area antagonizing me and degrading the job I was on. It really stirred my flesh up and maybe that's why he done it. I was very weak in this area of my life because I knew I had lost a lot in life and I wanted so badly to stand for something again. I went running around in the Plant blabbing my big mouth, telling all the machine operators I could run their job with my eyes close. And just to show them what I was talking about, I told them I was signing up for their job and then later the Supervisor job. They laughed as though, I was losing my mind but at this time I was dead serious. A funny thing happened right in the middle of that day. The Holy Spirit stopped me right in my tracks and told me, God had me there for a reason, and that was to teach me how to serve others and humble myself in the process.

This was another wake up call for me and I didn't take it lightly. I immediately changed my whole attitude with joy, it was a joy that came over me indescribable. From this day on I was a different worker in this place. My whole attitude had changed toward the people, no matter how they tried to ridicule me. Might of fact, when they said anything about me changing jobs for one of the better ones, I gave them such a pleasant answer of satisfaction, they stop asking me. I even went up to the guy who was antagonizing me so much and told him, God had spoke to me of my position in the plant and I apologized to him for getting out of character. Everyday after that, he would come in my area saying little things about christians and trying to let me know how much he knew about God. I just listened because in this area, I didn't have to prove anything because everything speaks for itself in the Bible. But one day he went a little too far, talking about what God expect and who satan was in the Bible. I tried to tell him to go to the scripture and read things for himself. Then I told him about the Holy Spirit and how the Holy Spirit helps a person understand the things of God. He simply told me, that stuff you're talking about is not real and it's just a myth. Right then, I told him, I didn't want to talk about it anymore because you're entering dangerous grounds now. I told him, be careful how you talk about the Holy Spirit because you're not hurting me but you're hurting yourself.

The following week when I came to work, this same guy had laid out from work and the next morning when I came in the parking lot of the job, he was sitting in the car with his mother crying and as I entered the work place, right away, some of the guys told me, he had just been terminated from his job. I really had sympathy for him, but I knew he had entered into dangerous grounds when he was talking about the Holy Spirit. My leadsman was telling everybody how this guy had got into it with me, and said, but look whose standing last. He was talking about things in the natural but I told him, he better be careful too, how you all speak against the things of God like it's a joke. God was really making transformation in my life again.

As time were going on, my mind was coming on too. One day, my girlfriend and I were out eating, when I seen a friend from one of the churches we used go to. She was a waitress in the place where we were eating, she met my girlfriend but it seemed like she was more concerned about me. She asked me was I going to church anywhere and I told her I was just going from church to church right now. Then I told her, "and that's not every Sunday". She mentioned to me about visiting her church and then reminded me of when she tried to get me to visit before. Then she handed me a cassette tape of one of the sermons from her pastor. I didn't think to much about it at this particular time but I told my girlfriend I think I will pay them a visit just to see what's going on over there. The following week I decided to go over to this church, since she had been persistent on getting me over there. I invited my girlfriend to go with me but she told me she just don't go to any churches like that, so I understood and went on.

My first Sunday over there blew my brains apart. This guy was on fire for the Lord. He was preaching and teaching a rhema word at the same time. It was like God had hooked me up with an Apostle similar in words as Apostle Paul's ministry. One of the first messages were about fornication and amongst other messages that filled my plate full. I was just astonished and amazed at this guy and how serious he was. I said to myself, I have to hear this guy again to make sure I'm not hallucinating. I went to hear him again and again, I couldn't stop because he was bringing the fresh living water Word straight from the Fountain of Life. God knew I needed a spiritual father right here on earth long before now. He(God) was right on time with this one because I really needed him now. God put me with a man of God that didn't play any games. He was bringing the Word so strong, I had to pray for him, that God gave him strength and endurance. I knew right then, if I sat under this man of God I had to straighten up and I knew God was ready to get me back on track and move me to a higher level in Christ.

When I came to work I had to talk about it and admit that I was wrong dealing with them while in the flesh. I told them, I went to a church that was on fire and now I knew as long as I stay obedient to God through this ministry, I'll regain the Spirit of God again. My girlfriend was telling me, I had changed since I've been going over to that church. I asked her to come over and hear what the man of God was saying, so we could be on the same page together. I told her, "if we are meant to be together, we need to be on the same page". She was getting angrier and angrier because I was cutting out all the things that caused us to be tempted. I finally quit having sex with her and was real with it and instead of dropping her cold turkey, I wanted her to come and join me. But she was totally against what I was doing. She even had the nerve to tell me something was wrong with that church, she said it seemed like a cult church. I told her, the only thing you may see is wrong is that they speak the truth and when the truth is told the adversary say it's a devil.

Things were really changing for me on my job and in my life. My attitude had changed and my confidence in the Holy Spirit was back. One night after Bible study, I was talking to a guy about how good God was doing in my life, when the Apostle past by me, I held out my hand to shake his hand and he did the same, except he bent down to touch my knees and demanded the spirit of Gout to come out of them. I laid on the floor receiving what he had spoke over my knees. After laying there about five to ten minutes, I got up with a new feeling in my knees and I jumped up and down on them with strength restored back in them. The amazing thing about this miracle was that I never told him about my knees. They had been hurting me so much I nearly needed a walking cane. I knew I had to lean on something every time I sat down or got up. I truly believed, since I had came into compromising with the world standards and had fallen back into sin. Satan had crepe in my body to attack my knees and whereas I was unaware of it because of my blindness. But as I speak to you today I haven't had any problem with them since the Apostle laid hands on them. I've never had this done on me, I've seen it done on others but never on me. Right then, I knew God was taking me to another level of faith, I praised the Lord and I praised the Lord, hallelujah. This was a special favor God sent through the Apostle, straight to me and by this I knew God was really using this man of God. I knew I was hooked up with the right team, I nearly told the whole world, sort of speaking. I told everybody I came in contact with, even my Supervisor and fellow workers. God was doing some great things before my eyes. He(God) even took the sting from my leadsman and humbled his spirit and his buddies. God took away my leadsman position and brought in another guy to take his job. And placed him down a notch with me. While humbling my spirit, God humbled his spirit also. Like the old saying, He killed two birds with one Stone. After this, everything were more pleasant and joyful at work. I prayed every day and still is for my spirit to remain humble, remain in humility and walk in meekness and plus, to have contentment with godliness. Last but not least, I pray for a full joy and to be filled with the Holy Spirit everyday and I ask God most of all to take away my anxiety as His Word say, be anxious for nothing. I found out that we might be walking around with the Holy Spirit but not enough of the Holy Spirit, Apostle Paul spoke on being filled with the Holy Spirit.

Now, my girlfriend wanted to come a long with me to the church after I finally put in my resignation with her. I told her, don't come because of my resignation but come because you want to be Saved. She came on to church with me and complained about a few things but she said she really like hearing the Apostle. She tried to tickle my ears with her words but my mind was already made up. She continued trying to get me to go to bed with her but I knew it was satan working through her more than herself. The rough thing about this situation was that she wouldn't take no for an answer. I couldn't get her or satan off my back for anything, so I could be able to go on with God's purpose for my life. Then I thought about my wife in which we had been separated for twenty years and had never been divorced. We managed to come back together and we tried it again for our children sakes and this brought a final closure to the old relationship with my girlfriend. My wife and I jumped back into each other without consideration of our lives from twenty years. I had checked the scriptures to make sure we were legal to do this. I went to 1 Corinthians 7: 11 and read about the woman being reconcile with her husband. So we went strong together for a while until she found out how serious I was in doing God's work. She simply told me we had different lifestyles and she didn't think it would work.

So here I was back in the middle wondering what direction to take now. I had left the church I was going to and now I was by myself again, alone with God. But the good thing about it this time was that I had matured in the spirit. I thought I was there at the church to stay but I think God just sent me there to be reconditioned. Because I learned how to intercede in prayer and I found out about a pride that Joseph had in the Old Testament that was similar to what I was carrying around. And later God placed me in a church with another whole level to let me know, He was still pushing me forward for His will to be done in my life. And I knew about satan's devices a lot more, and more than anything I knew about the demons of my own will and sometimes we have to fight the demons of our own will that sets in our minds.

When satan thinks he has you through temptation, it isn't anything better or more joyful than when God free you from this temptation. It brings joy to your soul, when you know God gave you the victory. When you lose your mind and I'm not talking about losing your mind and have to go to an asylum, no I'm talking about walking around with a lost mind and not knowing you've lost it. But God gives you your mind back, better than it was before, that's a joy, an unspeakable joy. I can praise God the rest of my life just for that. God is always moving us from hope to hope, faith to faith, and glory to glory. Martin Luther King said in one of his letters; During the tension of the heart of our nature, God don't judge us by the separate mistakes or incidents, but by the total bent of our lives. He said, life is sometimes like two head strong horses going in different directions but when we set out to build our dreams and to build our temples, we have to be determined. Then he said, God knows that His children are weak and He knows their frailties, that's why God requires that your heart is right, that's what God requires, that your heart is right.

When I first got out of jail with this new mind set, I promised myself I would be like the three mighty men of King Davids. I knew opposition were coming my way, so I wanted to be like the three mighty men. Where they fought until everything around them were subdued. This kind of strength comes from the Lord and we have to keep a strong will to continue on, no matter what comes our way. 2 Samuel 23:8-12, There were three mighty men whom David had:

> Adino the Eznite, had killed eight hundred men at one time. And after him was Eleazar the son of Dodo, the Ahohite, one of the three mighty men with David, when they defiled the Philistines, who gathered there for battle and the men of Israel had retreated. He arose and attacked the Philistines until his hand was weary, and his hand stuck to the sword. The Lord brought on a great victory that day and the people returned after him only to plunder. After him was Shammah the son of Agee the Hararite. The Philistines had gathered together into a troop where there was a piece of

ground full of lentils. So the people fled from the Philistines. But he
stationed himself in the middle of the field, defended it and killed
the Philistines. So the Lord brought about a great victory.

When all opposition comes our way and the forces get so strong, it
sometimes tries to take over, but we have to do what the three mighty men
did and that's to swing our sword, which is the Word of God, with all our
might and all our heart. And trust God for victory no matter what comes
our way. These men were great inspiration for me because they endured until
victory came and that's exactly what we have to do, no matter how hopeless it
seems. One thing I have learned, we have three major enemies coming after
us daily. One is life, which becomes burdensome sometimes, the second is
our flesh, which tries constantly to battle with our spirit. The last but not
lease is satan, who never lets up, he stays on our track. But the good thing to
know is that God left us with three powerful weapons; The Father, the Blood
of Jesus, and the Holy Spirit.

I just want to leave all of you with this scripture from Psalms 66:10-12;
For you, O God, have tested us; You have refined us as silver is refined.

You brought us into the net; You laid affliction on our backs. You have
caused men to ride over our heads; We went through fire and through water;
But You brought us out to rich fulfillment.

I can truly say that God's Word do not come back void, He allowed me
to place all my burdens on Him and taught me His ways, His life and His
truth. His Word stood in my life when He said come to me all who labor
and are heavy laden and I will give you rest. Take up My Yoke upon you and
learn from Me, for I am gentle and lowly in heart and you will find rest for
your souls. For My yoke is easy and My burden is light.